W9-BPL-235

BARRON'S DOG BIBLES

Shetland Sheepdogs

Sharon Vanderlip, DVM

BARRON'S

Acknowledgments

I thank my husband, Jack Vanderlip, DVM, for his valuable help as expert veterinary consultant and evaluator. Thanks so much for again taking care of our animals, tending to a never-ending list of home projects, working our practice, and tolerating a very messy house—making it possible for me to write another book! Thanks also to our daughter, Jacquelynn, for her help, enthusiasm, encouragement, and smiles. Without these two special people, this book could not have been completed. Special thanks are due to my friend of many years Lorraine Still of Robrovin Shelties, Sheltie and Collie judge and authority, for taking the time to share Sheltie stories and information with me.

This book is dedicated to all the Shelties that have won our hearts, to all the ethical Sheltie breeders who do their best to continually improve this wonderful breed, and to all the Shelties' owners who give their dogs the love and care they deserve.

And finally, this book honors the memory of Katie, a beautiful little Sheltie who gave my friend Karen many years of companionship and love.

About the Author

Sharon Vanderlip, DVM, has provided veterinary care to domestic and exotic animal species for more than 30 years. She has authored several books on dog breeds and animal care and published numerous articles for scientific, veterinary, and general reading audiences.

Dr. Vanderlip served as clinical veterinarian for the University of California San Diego School of Medicine and has collaborated on reproductive research projects with the San Diego Zoo. She is former chief of veterinary services for the National Aeronautics and Space Administration (NASA), and former chief of surgery for a large national institution specializing in reproductive medicine.

Dr. Vanderlip has lectured at kennel clubs and veterinary associations worldwide on topics in canine and exotic animal medicine. She has received awards for her writing and her dedication to animal health. She may be contacted at *www.sharonvanderlip.com*.

A Word About Pronouns

Many dog lovers feel that the pronoun "it" is not appropriate when referring to a pet that can be such a wonderful part of our lives. For this reason, Shetland Sheepdogs are described as "he" throughout this book unless the topic specifically relates to female dogs. This by no means infers any preference, nor should it be taken as an indication that either sex is particularly problematic.

Cover Credits

Shutterstock: back cover; Sharon Vanderlip: front cover.

Photo Credits

Barbara Augello: pages 162, 178, 182; Gerry Bucsis/ Barbara Somerville: pages 40, 160; Seth Casteel: pages 5, 19, 39, 58, 69; DrsFosterSmith.com: page 159; Cheryl Ertelt: pages 18, 32, 68, 126, 167; Dreamstime.com: page 42; iStockphoto: pages 16, 34, 49, 54, 64, 76, 85, 89, 148; Jeanmfogle.com: pages 105, 112, 156; Paulette Johnson: pages 31, 37, 60, 71, 83; Daniel Johnson: pages 121, 132 (top), 132 (bottom), 133 (top), 133 (bottom), 134 (top), 134 (bottom), 135 (top), 135 (bottom), 136 (top), 136 (bottom), 137 (top), 137 (bottom); Lisa Kruss: pages 74, 102, 108; MaxDogPhoto.com: pages 9, 116, 128, 129; Shutterstock: pages vi, 6, 14, 23, 24, 29, 45, 53, 67, 79, 86, 99, 103, 107, 120, 122, 169, 171, 174, 186; Steve Surfman: page 118; Sharon Vanderlip: pages i, iii, 2, 10, 11, 12, 22, 62, 90, 92, 93, 96, 111, 124, 138, 140, 143, 145, 147 (top), 147 (bottom), 149, 150.

© Copyright 2012 by Barron's Educational Series, Inc.

All rights reserved.
No part of this publication may be reproduced or distributed in any form or by any means without the written permission of the copyright owner.

All inquiries should be addressed to:
Barron's Educational Series, Inc.
250 Wireless Boulevard
Hauppauge, New York 11788
www.barronseduc.com

ISBN: 978-0-7641-8678-3 (DVD)
ISBN: 978-1-4380-7216-6 (Package)

Library of Congress Catalog Card No: 2012002946

Library of Congress Cataloging-in-Publication Data
Vanderlip, Sharon Lynn
    Shetland Sheepdogs/ Sharon Vanderlip
        p.cm. — (Barron's dog bibles)
    Includes index.
        ISBN 978-1-4380-7216-6 — ISBN 978-0-7641-8673-3
        1. Shetland sheepdog. I. Title.
SF429. S62V36 2012
636.7′1—dc23   2012002946

Printed in China

9 8 7 6 5 4 3 2 1

CONTENTS

CONTENTS

PREFACE

The Sheltie is a *working* dog: hardy, muscular, well proportioned, balanced, energetic. For centuries the Sheltie's ancestors were selected and bred for strength and stamina to perform demanding and complicated work. Shelties had to be able to learn quickly, understand and follow commands, focus on the job, solve problems, be determined, and adapt to rapidly changing situations. Above all, Shelties had to be "biddable," meaning they had to be obedient, docile, and eager to do what was asked of them.

In the early development of the Shetland Sheepdog breed, working ability took precedence over appearance. It is hard to imagine that appearance wasn't the first consideration when we see that today Shelties are among the most beautiful dog breeds in existence! Sometimes called a "miniature Collie," Shelties are related to Collies, but they are not the product of breeding undersized Collies together. Shelties have their own unique set of ancestors, which include other types of dogs introduced to the Shetland Islands throughout the centuries.

Today, the Shetland Sheepdog ranks among the most popular breeds worldwide. In addition to their exquisite beauty, Shelties are widely recognized for their high level of working intelligence, consistently ranking among the top 10 breeds earning the most obedience awards.

It's not surprising that you are drawn to the Shetland Sheepdog. Like countless others, you may have first fallen for the Sheltie's charm because of its beauty and exuberant personality. Or, perhaps you couldn't resist the gorgeous coat. Or, you may have found the Sheltie's small size appealing and suitable to your lifestyle. But spend just a little time with a Sheltie and you soon realize that the true treasure lies in the complex workings of this extraordinary dog's mind, its keen devotion to its human family, its intelligence, its intense desire to work and to please, and its remarkable communication skills.

Shelties are very finely attuned to the moods, desires, and emotions of their owners. They are not independent dogs. They want to be with, work for, and please their people all the time. Shelties love to work and to learn. They were carefully selected and bred for these qualities for generations, so it's in their genes. Shelties are intensely loyal dogs that bond very closely with their owners. Partnership and communication are as important today, in Sheltie ownership and in living with a Sheltie, as they were more than a century ago.

Whether you already own a Shetland Sheepdog or are considering adding one to your life, this book gives you the valuable information you need to understand how your Sheltie thinks, his innate behaviors, and how to communicate with him. This book will also help you give your Sheltie the very best of care and ensure that he is healthy and happy throughout his life.

Chapter One

All About Shetland Sheepdogs

The Shetland Sheepdog is the quintessential canine: affectionate, intelligent, good-natured, willing, intensely loyal, and beautiful. It is, above all, a *close companion* and a *working dog*. When we admire our Shelties, we cannot help but appreciate the dedicated efforts of Shetland Sheepdog breeders. In little more than a century, through careful selective breeding, the Sheltie has blossomed from a small farm dog of variable type and mixed ancestry to a stunning beauty with an impressive pedigree, remarkable intelligence, and the proven ability to excel in a wide range of competitive activities.

Certainly, the Shetland Sheepdog has come a very long way from its humble beginnings in the remote Shetland Islands, where its ancestors were used as working farm dogs to herd, gather, and protect sheep. Out of the hundreds of dog breeds in existence today, the Shetland Sheepdog ranks among the most popular breeds worldwide. The Sheltie's immense appeal is due in large part to its alert, sweet expression; gentle nature; small size; and glamorous coat. These attributes are surpassed only by the Sheltie's high trainability, eagerness to please, and keen devotion to its human family.

Research studies have ranked the Shetland Sheepdog among the most intelligent of breeds in learning ability, memory, and problem solving. Shelties feature prominently on the list of title winners in a large variety of competitive events, including obedience, agility, herding, and conformation. But arguably the Sheltie's greatest attribute is its uncanny ability to understand and communicate with its owners. The Shetland Sheepdog is endowed with all of the most desirable qualities we seek in a canine companion. Little wonder that the Sheltie tugs on our heartstrings like no other dog can.

A Brief History

The more we know about the Shetland Sheepdog's history, the more we understand and appreciate our own Shelties. A review of the breed's history teaches us about the environment and conditions in which the Sheltie

Fun Facts

DNA Revelations

When researchers studied the canine genome, they also studied the genetic relationship between various breeds. They found that all of the herding dogs were grouped together, meaning they were all very closely related and they all came from the same "branch" of the canine family tree.

originated, as well as the kind of work and stamina demanded of our Shelties' ancestors. The criteria that were used to select dogs to serve the farmers' needs and delight dog fanciers are the same criteria that eventually led to the development of the Shetland Sheepdog as a distinct and popular breed. This information is valuable, because for countless canine generations, the traits that were considered so highly desirable at the onset of the breed's evolution have been genetically concentrated in each subsequent generation. Inside and out—from your Sheltie's physical appearance, to his innermost mental workings, and everything in between—all are directly linked to your Sheltie's history: his ancestry and the consistent selection for specific attributes, abilities, and behaviors.

The Sheltie's *written* history is somewhat limited before its recognition as a distinct breed in the early 1900s. Fortunately, the Sheltie's ancient history is indelibly recorded on something more permanent than paper. It is embedded in fossil bones and fixed in genetic material (DNA) that scientists are able to read and interpret today. Science has recently provided some surprising answers to many of the mysteries that have enshrouded the Sheltie for so long. So let's travel back in time to learn how our Shetland Sheepdog came to be.

Wild Ancestry

The Sheltie's sweet expression and gentle demeanor belie the fact that, like all members of the domestic dog species (known as *Canis familiaris*), the Shetland Sheepdog is a direct descendant of the gray wolf and shares 98.2 percent of its genetic material in common with this very close wild ancestor.

Dogs were the first animals to be domesticated by humans, although precisely when and where are still topics of lively debate. Archeologists contend that the fossil evidence places canine evolution somewhere between 13,000 and 17,000 years ago. The study of mitochondrial DNA sequences (genetic material that remain relatively unchanged through maternal lineage) has suggested as much as 100,000 years of domestication. Some scientists are comfortable with a time frame of 40,000 years, which falls somewhere between the fossil and genetic data. Clearly, to date, there are conflicting data and there is some disagreement, but with more studies and as we continue to gather new information, the pieces to the canine puzzle will eventually fit together. As for the location of domestication, mitochondrial DNA studies indicated it began in East Asia, but a more recent and extensive survey of the canine genome points instead to the Middle East. DNA also tells us that there was more than one domestication "event." In other words, domestication likely occurred at different times in different areas with local strains of wolves.

Breed Truths

The early Shelties and their ancestors were known by several names:

Toonie* Dog
Toonie Collie
Peerie Dog
Fairy Dog
Lilliputian Collie
Miniature Collie
Shetland Collie**

*The word *Toonie* is thought to have been derived from "town" or "township" and/or from the Tun dog, introduced by the Vikings and thought to be a possible ancestor of the Sheltie.
**Collies and Shelties are two distinct breeds. Shelties were not created by repeatedly breeding small or undersized Collies. Collie breeders insisted that when the Sheltie was officially named, the word *Collie* be replaced with *Sheepdog*.

Fun Facts

Why didn't crofters keep detailed written records of their dogs' lineage in the early history of the breed? Maybe they didn't have all the information or didn't have enough time for paperwork. Farmers selected their dogs according to temperament and working ability more than what they reflected on paper.

Keeping track of one generation (two parents), two generations (two parents and four grandparents), or even three generations (add eight great-grandparents) is manageable, but the farther back in a dog's pedigree (family tree) one goes, the more names and details there are to record. A 30-year time span could represent at least 10 canine generations. Twenty generations represent more than one million (1,048,576) dog names to record. Thirty generations would be more than one billion dog names (1,073,741,824). So, we see that keeping track of dog pedigrees can be a daunting task. We also know that billions of dogs did not inhabit the Shetland Islands. Obviously, a large number (most) of the dogs used for breeding on the Shetland Islands were already closely related. This means that the same ancestors would have appeared multiple times on a single dog's pedigree. This is, in fact, how breeds are created.

Placing canine domestication in the Middle East also correlates with when humans' first settled communities began to appear in the Middle East 15,000 years ago. Most scientists agree that dogs had a complex impact on the structure of human society and enabled humans to shift away from their hunter-gathering lifestyle to one of agriculture and farming.

History and Development

At some remote point in time, domesticated dogs were introduced to the Shetland Islands. Most dog breeds today are the result of human intervention over a period of one to three centuries. The *earliest written history* specifically pertaining to the Shetland Sheepdog and its ancestry dates from the late nineteenth and early twentieth centuries. This history is, for the most part, a compilation of writings by a few early pioneers of the breed relating what they knew from firsthand experience, what they thought, and what they were told by others. There were no official registries for sheepdogs before 1870. Sheepdogs were simply identified by their regions and their working style.

The Shetland Islands farmers (also referred to as crofters) selected dogs for companionship, working ability, and their adaptation to the terrain and climate in which they had to work. Crofters did not take the time to keep detailed breeding records, nor were they interested in doing so. Indeed, keeping track of specifics pertaining to dogs involved in breeding programs (names, numbers, characteristics, colors) is an enormous task. The Sheltie's ancestors were anonymous working dogs, without pedigrees. Fortunately, when the Shetland Sheepdog was recognized as a distinct breed, record keeping became an important part of the breed's history.

A Working and Herding Dog

The dogs of the Shetland Islands were reportedly an interesting concoction of canine bloodlines selected primarily for their working ability, intelligence, small size, and stamina to do the hard work required of them.

Breed Truths

According to historians, Shetland Sheepdogs were preferred for herding Shetland sheep because the island sheep were small, wild, and agile, and a small Sheltie was well suited for the job and did not consume as much food as a large dog.

According to collective writings of the early proponents of the breed in the early 1900s and breed historians, it is believed that some of the Sheltie's early ancestors were small Spitz-type dogs originating from Scandinavia. These dogs were presumably introduced when Norsemen colonized the Shetland Islands, neighboring Orkney Islands, and Scotland in the late eighth and ninth centuries. Some authors have credited the King Charles Spaniel and the Pomeranian as being part of the Shetland Sheepdog's hereditary blend. Unfortunately, we cannot know for sure how much of the information passed down to us is accurate and how much is speculation.

James Loggie, a resident of the Shetland Islands and the first secretary of the Shetland Collie Club (established 1908), wrote that whalers from Greenland brought "Yakki" dogs to the Shetland Islands. According to Loggie, the "Yakki" dogs were crossed with the resident working dogs and mixed working collie-type-dogs. Loggie added that Collie mixes and "Scotch Collies" were brought to the Shetland Islands from the mainland and interbred with the island dogs.

Dogs were raised on the Shetland Islands for companionship, herding, and protection. Survival of the flock—and ultimately the farmer's livelihood—depended largely on a dog's ability to keep the sheep safe and gathered. Sheepherding was difficult and complicated work in the Shetland Islands. Shelties had to adapt to challenging and changing situations. Most of the land was not fenced or enclosed, so it was up to the dogs to keep the sheep from straying and to chase away predators that could harm the flock. The dogs' long list of responsibilities included keeping the sheep away from the garden and feed-storage areas, gathering the flock together, herding sheep back out to pasture, and herding the sheep back again when it was time to shear them. When there was a possible threat or danger, the dogs would bark warnings to alert the farmer. For a small farm dog to manage such a big job called for an extraordinary mixture of intelligence, endurance, willingness, and comprehension. The Sheltie had to be sturdy, muscular, hardy, agile, and have plenty of stamina to accomplish such demanding work. It also had to be able to learn quickly, understand commands, and excel at communicating and working *in partnership* with its handler. Above all, the Sheltie had to be *biddable*, meaning it had to be obedient and acquiescent and do its handlers' biddings quickly and willingly.

Sheltie Time Line

During the Victorian era, hobby breeding and developing new breeds became increasingly popular. Dog ownership was a fashionable luxury and a status symbol in many circles. Small breeds were especially popular. Loggie was among the first Sheltie advocates to recognize that the small, loyal, multitalented Sheltie had a bright future on and *off* the farm, at home and abroad. Loggie and others joined to actively promote the breed. From that time on, Sheltie history was more carefully recorded.

Starting around 1896, Shelties were exhibited in Lerwick, the capital of the Shetland Islands, where Loggie resided. Early breeders acknowledged that many of the dogs were not consistent in type, but they also knew that their little island dogs were living gems. They decided it was time to create a breed standard and seek breed recognition for their beloved Shetland Sheepdogs.

Oddy, another early proponent of the Sheltie, wrote that except for their heads and ears, the Shetland Island dogs were "replicas of the modern Collie." Breeders agreed that the Shetland Sheepdog should ideally resemble a "Collie in miniature." To accomplish this goal, they introduced more Collie bloodlines into the lineages and improved many qualities, especially as they pertained to head and skull, profuse coat, and herding instinct. Loggie stressed in his writings that any Shelties showing signs of "spaniel," or rounded or domed skulls, should not be used for breeding and was adamant that Collie character be maintained— but breeders soon learned that creating the ideal Shetland Sheepdog was challenging. It wasn't easy to keep their dogs consistent in type *and* preserve small size. Collies were taller and heavier than Shetland Sheepdogs, and by introducing more Collie genes, breeders found that it was also more difficult to keep the Shelties within the smaller, desirable size range. To this day, we still see some Shelties that grow larger than the ideal standard.

Fun Facts

Collie Confusion!

The Shetland Sheepdog's ancestors did not look like miniatures of the alluring rough Collie that you see in the show ring today! There appear to be several origins and definitions of the word *Collie*. One source tells us that it is a Gaelic word for "useful" and so it was used to describe herding dogs of any type, color, or markings. Another source reports that this is also the word for "puppy" in one form of Gaelic. Some authors say that black-face sheep were called "collies" or "colleys" and so the dogs that worked the black-faced sheep were called "collie dogs" or "colley dogs." We are also told that *Coll* means "black" in Anglo-Saxon and that *Coll*, *Coaly*, and *Coally* (perhaps in reference to black coal) may have been used to describe black sheepdogs. Collie has also been suggested as a descriptive term for "collar", as in the white collar seen in many Shelties and Collies today.

FYI: Famous Shelties

- English/American Champion Helensdale Laddie: the first Sheltie in America to hold both English and American Championship titles (he lived to be 18 years old!)
- Champion Wee Lassie of Eve-Bart, UD: the first champion to be the nation's top obedience dog
- OT Champion Malcolm MacDuff, UDX: the first Sheltie to win the AKC National Obedience Invitational Tournament
- American/Canadian Champion Olympic Fairy Flower: the first Sheltie with an Obedience title to also win a Best in Show
- Halstor's Peter Pumpkin: the Sheltie who sired the most champions
- Reveille II: the official mascot of Texas A & M University from 1952 to 1966

In 1908, the Shetland Collie Club was established in Lerwick. The club wrote a standard for the breed, saying that the Shetland Sheepdog should be similar to a "rough Collie in miniature" and that height should not exceed 15 inches (38 cm). The following year, the Scottish Shetland Collie Club formed, maintaining their own stud book and registry. Their standard indicated that the Sheltie should look like "an ordinary Collie in miniature," about 12 inches (30.5 cm) high, weighing 10 to 14 pounds (4.5 to 6.4 kg), and smooth (short-haired) and rough (long-haired) varieties were allowed. However, shortly afterward, the smooth Sheltie was "banned" from inclusion in the final standard.

In 1914, the Shetland Sheepdog received breed recognition from the English Kennel Club. Shelties were initially registered as Shetland Collies, but because of protests from Collie breeders, the name was changed later in the year to Shetland Sheepdogs. That same year the English Shetland Collie Club formed, known today as the English Shetland Sheepdog Club.

Fun Facts

Collie Word Controversy

Collie breeders were displeased with the use of the word *Collie* in naming and recognition of the Sheltie as a distinct breed. They insisted that the word *Collie* be replaced with *Sheepdog*— and so the Sheltie's name was changed from Shetland Collie to Shetland Sheepdog.

Shelties in America

On the other side of the Atlantic, the first Sheltie imports arrived in 1907, and an article about them appeared in the *Boston Globe* in 1909. Shelties received additional publicity in an article that appeared in *Dogdom Magazine*

in 1911, the same year the breed was acknowledged and accepted by the American Kennel Club (AKC). By 1913, 12 Shelties had already found their way to the American show ring, and in 1914, 6 Shelties were exhibited at the venerable Westminster Show. Reports say that these first representa-

Fun Facts

The first Shetland Sheepdog to receive a championship was Champion Woodvold in 1913. According to historians, her mother was a Collie.

Breed Truths

During World War I, the Shetland Sheepdog population dropped perilously low. The mid 1920s saw a significant increase in Sheltie importations to America. Sheltie breeding was also limited during World War II. Since WWII there have been no influential imports or exports between the United States and United Kingdom. From the 1950s on, Sheltie numbers and popularity rose steadily. Today the Sheltie ranks among the top 20 most popular breeds in the United States.

tives were not uniform in type, but nevertheless, the Sheltie had found a place in America's heart and was here to stay. The American Shetland Sheepdog Association was founded in 1929.

Note: For an extensive and detailed history of individual Shetland Sheepdogs, breeders, and famous kennels in the United States, refer to McGowan (see Resources).

Characteristics

The Shetland Sheepdog is first and foremost a *companion*. Shelties are not independent dogs. They originated in remote areas where they did not encounter many people and were carefully selected for special attributes, including their deep loyalty. Shelties bond closely with their owners and are very affectionate and responsive to them. But the Sheltie doesn't give its heart away to strangers. It is often aloof or reserved around strangers, yet watchful, until it has had a chance to become sufficiently acquainted—at its own pace and in its own time. Shelties are gentle, well-mannered, willing dogs with a sound disposition. They should not be aggressive, shy, nervous, snappy, or stubborn.

The Shetland Sheepdog is a herding dog, and as such it is an alert, active, energetic athlete. Many Shelties retain the strong herding instinct of their forebears. This is only natural, as it has been bred into them for generations. It is part of their genetic makeup. Shelties can be very vocal barkers, especially while performing activities or excited at play. In addition to herding livestock, Shelties may also try to herd family members, especially children, or even herd other family pets. Some Shelties can be inclined to nip while herding.

The Shetland Sheepdog Breed Standard for the United States and for the United Kingdom are similar. The standards are highly detailed, describing the "ideal" Sheltie at length. The complete breed standards can be found on the corresponding websites (for the United States: the American Kennel Club [*www.akc.org*] or the American Shetland Sheepdog Association [*www.assa.org*] and for the United Kingdom: Kennel Club [*www.the-kennel-club.org/uk*] and English Shetland Sheepdog Club [*www.essc.org/uk*]).

The standard describes the Sheltie as a well-muscled, sturdy, lithe, agile, and beautiful dog that is well proportioned, sound, and balanced.

The Sheltie's head is described as elegant and refined, having a long, blunt wedged shape that tapers from the ears to the nose. The top of the skull is flat, as are the cheeks that merge smoothly into a full, well-rounded muzzle. The jaw is powerful with a well-developed underjaw. The teeth are even and fit together in a "scissors bite" and should all be present. Lips are tight, not sagging, and the nose is black. The top of the skull and the top of the muzzle are parallel planes of equal length. The difference in height between the top of the skull and the top of the muzzle results in a slight, but definite "stop" where skull and muzzle meet. The balance point is the inner corner of the eyes. The eyes are medium sized with almond-shaped rims, and set somewhat obliquely in the skull. The ears are small and placed high on the head with the tip breaking forward. In repose, the ears are folded back into the frill. Head shape, together with ear set, eye placement, and dark eye color, all combine in such a way as to produce a sweet, alert, inquisitive, and intelligent expression.

Fun Facts

To improve consistency of type in the Shetland Sheepdog, Shelties were crossed with show Collies in the breed's very early history. Although not all crosses were documented, it is estimated that Shetland Sheepdogs in the United States today share at least 50 percent of their bloodlines in common with Collies. Authorities contend that some Shetland Sheepdogs in the United Kingdom today may have up to 90 percent Collie bloodlines behind them.

The Sheltie's neck is well muscled and arched to carry the head proudly. The body is strong and well muscled, with a deep chest and well-sprung ribs. The abdomen is tucked up, and the muscular back is level, with the croup sloping gradually to the rear. Thighs are well muscled, hocks are

short and straight, and forelimbs are straight and muscular. Correct structure and angulation of the limbs allow for freedom of movement, speed, and agility. The feet are oval and compact with well-padded, arched toes that fit together tightly. A Sheltie's gait is effortless, smooth, and graceful with strong drive from the hindquarters. The tail is sufficiently long that the last bone in the tail touches the hock joint. At rest, the tail is carried low but may have a slight upward curve. The tail should not curve up over the back.

The Sheltie carries a profuse double coat. The outer coat is harsh, straight, and long. It should not be curly, wavy, soft, or silky. The undercoat is short, furry, and dense. The forelegs are well feathered, hind legs above the hocks have a profuse amount of hair, and the mane and frill are abundant, especially in males. Hair on the face, ear tips, and feet, and below the hock is smooth.

Breed Truths

Why do some Shelties grow taller than the standard describes? Scientists have mapped the canine genome and have found some answers. Researchers have identified genes in the dog that play a role in determining size. When early breeders crossed their Shelties with Collies to make Shelties look like "miniature rough show Collies," they also introduced the genes for larger size.

FYI: Genetics

The genetics of Shetland Sheepdog eye and coat color inheritance is a very complicated subject. For example, blue-merle coloration is caused by a specific gene acting on a black coat to dilute the color and cause merling. The gene for merling also acts on a sable coat. Sable-merles often have a paler coat color, and merling may be evident only when the Sheltie is a puppy or upon close inspection. Like blue-merles, sable-merles may have blue coloration in their eyes. The gene for merling and the gene for bi-color are different genes that are inherited separately. Genetically, the bi-black is recessive to the tricolor. There are also genes that control the amount of white markings on the coat. A gene for white-factoring (a piebald gene) can cause extensive conspicuous white body spots and extensive white markings, which disqualify a Sheltie from the show ring. The gene for white factoring and the merle gene are different genes that are inherited separately. White puppies resulting from the white-factor gene always have fully colored heads, may have colored body spots, and are not defective. White-merle puppies (*homozygous* merle) resulting from two merle parents do not have fully colored heads and may have vision problems (including extremely small, under-developed, or even missing eyes) and/or hearing problems (such as poor hearing or total deafness in one or both ears).

Size

The U.S. Shetland Sheepdog Breed Standard limits size between 13 inches (33 cm) and 16 inches (40.6 cm) at the shoulder. The U.K. Shetland Sheepdog Breed Standard sets the height limit to 14½ inches (37 cm) at the shoulder with only an inch (2.5 cm) leeway above or below the ideal.

Accepted Colors and Markings

Markings:

- White markings may appear on the Sheltie's face, collar, legs, feet, and tip of tail.
- Tan markings may appear on the Sheltie's cheeks, above the eyes, and on the legs.

Color:

- Sable: Includes colors ranging in intensity from golden to deep mahogany plus white markings
- Black: Includes tricolors and bi-blacks
- Tricolor: Predominantly black with tan markings and white markings

Fun Facts

It is believed that the Shetland Sheepdog acquired the gene for merling from the Collie. Scientists have identified the merle gene in the canine genome, and it is being studied extensively.

- Bi-black (also called bi-color): Predominantly black with white markings but without tan markings
- Blue-merle: Predominantly silvery-blue-gray with black merling (mottling or marbling) with tan markings and white markings
- Bi-Blue: Predominantly silvery-blue-gray with black merling with white markings but without tan markings
- Brindle coloration is not allowed.

Fun Facts

The dog is the only species to have the gene for merling. The merle gene is limited to only a few breeds, including the Shetland Sheepdog and its close relative, the Collie.

FYI: American Kennel Club Group Classifications

Group I	Sporting Dogs	Border Collie
Group II	Hounds	Bouvier des Flandres
Group III	Working Dogs	Briard
Group IV	Terriers	Canaan Dog
Group V	Toys	Cardigan Welsh Corgi
Group VI	Non-Sporting Dogs	Collie
Group VII	**Herding Dogs**	Entlebucher Mountain Dog
Miscellaneous Class		German Shepherd Dog
		Icelandic Sheepdog
Group VII: Herding Dogs		Norwegian Buhund
Australian Cattle Dog		Old English Sheepdog
Australian Shepherd		Pembroke Welsh Corgi
Bearded Collie		Polish Lowland
Beauceron		Puli
Belgian Malinois		Pyrenean Shepherd
Belgian Sheepdog		**Shetland Sheepdog**
Belgian Tervuren		Swedish Vallhund

Eye color:
Preferred eye color is dark brown.

Note: It is possible for merle Shelties to have brown eyes, brown eyes with blue coloration, blue eyes, or one blue and one brown eye. Sable Shelties with any blue coloration in their eyes are genetically sable-merles. Blue-eyed sable-colored Shelties are not accepted in the show ring.

Genetics and Coat Color Inheritance

The genetics of coat color inheritance is too complicated for the scope of this book, but excellent coat color inheritance charts, explanations, and information may be found in books (see "Resources": Vanderlip, and McKinney and Rleseberg). In addition, intensive research is being conducted on the merle gene, as well as its interaction with the piebald gene, and this research has led to recent publications (see "Resources": Clark et al. and Vanderlip).

Breed Truths

Not a Toy

The Shetland Sheepdog is *not* a toy breed. It is *not* a dwarf or under-sized Collie. Shelties and Collies are closely related and share some common ancestors, but they are different breeds.

Chapter Two

The Mind of the Shetland Sheepdog

The Shetland Sheepdog is best recognized for his beauty, intelligence, and versatility, but it is his *character* that makes this canine so special and sets him apart from other breeds. Your Sheltie's character is a combination of his temperament and his personality. Together they form the integral framework of your Sheltie's mind.

Sheltie Temperament

Temperament is an inherited trait. A sound temperament can blossom to its full genetic potential, or it can wither, depending on how well the Sheltie is nurtured, raised, and trained. Inherited traits—combined with sensory input, past experiences, intelligence level, and even memories—are important elements that together influence how this extraordinary canine thinks and behaves and how his personality develops.

Compared with many breeds, the Shetland Sheepdog has a short recorded history. His list of known pedigrees are limited to this past century, and the accuracy of some of the early breeding records is questionable. But researchers have confirmed, through DNA analysis, that the Sheltie descends, in large part, from the early working Collie-type dog. We know that show Collies were crossed with Shelties in the early twentieth century and that show Collies are also descendants of the early working Collie-type dog. This means that adding Collie bloodlines to the existing Shetland Sheepdog gene pool further reinforced working and herding dog traits in the breed.

Breed Truths

Excerpt from the Shetland Sheepdog standard from the American Kennel Club:

Temperament
The Shetland Sheepdog is intensely loyal, affectionate, and responsive to his owner. However, he may be reserved toward strangers but not to the point of showing fear or cringing in the ring. *Faults—* Shyness, timidity, or nervousness. Stubbornness, snappiness, or ill temper.

The Shetland Sheepdog is the product of *selective breeding* over the past century, with an emphasis on obtaining and retaining the highly desirable traits of a working and herding dog. These qualities include sound temperament, high intelligence, working ability, trustworthiness, loyalty, willingness, and an intense desire to please. The Shetland Sheepdog possesses all of these qualities and more. The Shetland Sheepdog is endowed with a superb character, high intelligence, beauty, and the true mind-set of a working and herding dog.

By the time the Shetland Sheepdog was officially recognized as a distinct breed, his temperament was well established. Temperament is such an important part of the Shetland Sheepdog's character that the breed standard specifically faults Shelties that have "ill temper."

Breed Truths

Shelties are confident and self-assured. They should never be shy or aggressive. When in the presence of strangers, Shelties may be friendly, or calm and observant, or often even casually aloof until they get to know a person. Most Shelties are not quick to give their trust or affection to strangers. Instead they reserve that for their owners. Strangers have to earn it!

Sheltie Personality

Every Sheltie's personality is influenced by a variety of factors, including his experiences and interactions with people and other animals, his socialization, learning, and training, and the age at which these events occur.

The first 12 weeks of a Sheltie's life are the most critical and impressionable when it comes to personality development, especially between the ages of 3 and 9 weeks of age. Some of your Sheltie's behavior is instinctive, but because he bonds so closely with you and is so sensitive and responsive to your moods and cues, a great deal of his personality and behavior will be influenced by you and his home environment.

Fun Facts

Shelties rank among the most intelligent and versatile of all dog breeds! The first Sheltie obedience titlist was only 11 months old and had received only three weeks of training before the competition. Beach Cliff's Lizette later went on to be the first Sheltie to earn a UD title. Ch. Merry Memory of Pocano was one of the first CDX winners in the United States. Shelties continue to be among the top winning breeds for top honors in a wide variety of events.

There are two additional important periods in a Sheltie's developmental stages during which socialization and exposure to people, places, and things are very important. These periods are sometimes called the *fear imprint*

PERSONALITY POINTERS
Sheltie Personality

Normal Sheltie Personality	Sheltie Problem Behavior
Confident, interested, calm	Fearful of situations, nervous, flighty
Friendly but reserved and watchful with kind, gentle eye expression; may also be aloof; interested and not fearful, never aggressive	Fearful or shy of strangers or new situations, tries to hide or run away
Compatible with people and other dogs	Aggressive
Calm, responsive	Hyperactive
Stable, consistent, even tempered	Unpredictable: overly friendly one moment, frightened, nervous, or unfriendly the next moment
Trustworthy, reliable, nonaggressive	Fear-biter or aggressive
Barks for expression and reasons Note: Most Shelties love to bark and are naturally vociferous.	Excessive problem barking
Seeks approval and wants to please	Is not eager to please, unwilling

periods, and they occur between 8 and 11 weeks of age and again later at 6 to 14 months of age. During this time it is very important to make sure your Sheltie is exposed to people, sounds, smells, places, and activities in a positive way and is rewarded for calm, good, outgoing, confident behavior.

The Sheltie is a quick learner and an independent thinker. Although originally selected for driving and herding livestock, today's Shetland Sheepdog is extremely versatile and adaptable (see Chapter 7, "Training and Activities"). You will be amazed by your Sheltie's extraordinary reasoning and problem-solving abilities.

Shelties rank very high in intelligence. In one study, they learned and obeyed commands faster than almost all other breeds of dogs tested (see "Resources"). Shelties are dynamic, energetic, and enthusiastic. Everything they do, they do with flair. They love to work and they love to please. They consistently win top honors in a wide range of competitions, such as obedience, agility, flyball, and herding. They also perform well in many services, including police scent work, search and rescue, and therapy dog work. It takes a high level of intelligence, keen reasoning, and the ability to focus

ACTIVITIES Preventing Boredom

It is a joy to own a highly intelligent dog, but it is also a challenge. Shelties are naturally inquisitive and constantly learning as they explore and seek out new information, situations, and activities. Shelties like to do things! If your Sheltie does not receive enough of your time and attention, or enough training and activities, he will become bored and can get into mischief. That's when good Shelties may do bad things. If left alone, isolated and with nothing to entertain him, your Sheltie may chew and destroy objects or bark. Here are some ways to help your Sheltie avoid boredom:

- Spend lots of time with your Sheltie every day and play with him. He will bond closely with you and thrive on your companionship.
- Do not leave your Sheltie alone for long periods of time.
- Give your Sheltie the exercise he needs and take him on regular, frequent walks and outings.
- Provide your Sheltie with mental stimulation such as challenging fun games and interesting toys.
- Train your Sheltie every day. Training never ends, and Shelties continue to learn throughout their lives.
- Keep activities and training varied, fun, and limited to a reasonable amount of time so that they remain interesting for both of you.
- Use positive reinforcement and rewards for your Sheltie with lots of praise and affection.

and concentrate on a goal to be so successful in these endeavors. Yet Shelties make it look easy.

Your Sheltie is the product of more than a century of careful *selection*. The result is a beautiful, loyal, intelligent, highly trainable, happy, good-natured, confident dog that loves to work and is eager to please you. No wonder Shelties are so popular throughout the world!

Sheltie Senses

Shelties have very keen senses, especially compared with humans. All of your Sheltie's sensory input is processed in his brain and plays a role in how he responds to various situations.

Sense of Smell

Of all your Sheltie's senses, he relies most on his keen sense of smell to give him

Breed Truths

It is not unusual for a Sheltie to choose one family member as his "special person" and favor that individual with more affection.

information about the world around him. A Sheltie is equipped with close to 200 million olfactory receptor cells (humans have about 5 million olfactory receptor cells) and an olfactory ability estimated to be up to 1 million times more efficient than that of a human. Many Shelties are successful in tracking competitions and in assisting in police work and search and recovery.

Breed Truths

Shetland Sheepdogs are highly tuned in to their owners and take their cues from them. If the owner is high strung, nervous, or shy, this can cause the dog to become apprehensive and to behave in the same manner. Shyness and nervousness are highly undesirable character flaws in a Sheltie. If the owner is calm and confident, then the dog will feel secure and confident as well.

Sense of Taste

Your Sheltie's sense of taste is closely linked to his sense of smell. Dogs have fewer taste buds than humans (about 1,700 buds in dogs, compared with approximately 9,000 taste buds in humans) and most dogs' taste buds are clustered near the tip of the tongue. Dogs can taste bitter, sweet, salt, and sour. In addition, dogs have a vomeronasal organ at the roof of their mouths. This organ enables dogs to "taste" smells and sends the sensory information to the limbic system of the brain, which is responsible for many emotional responses. Much, if not most, of a Sheltie's sense of food enjoyment is linked to the way the food smells.

FYI: Through Shelties Eyes

The Color You See	The Color Your Sheltie May See
Violet	Dark Blue
Blue	Light Blue
Blue Green	Gray
Green	Light Yellow
Yellow	Dark Yellow to Brown
Orange	Yellow
Red	Dark Gray to Black

Sight

Shelties see differently from humans. Their peripheral vision is better than that of a human being, and they are able to detect moving objects better. This is very useful for a working dog that must be fast and accurate. However, the Sheltie's depth perception and visual acuity is not as keen as that of humans. Shelties have better night vision than humans do, but they cannot see colors as we do. This is because they have only two kinds of cone cells. Cone cells in the eyes respond to different wavelengths of light, and the brain processes the information as perceived color. Humans have three kinds of cone cells and can see a wide range of colors. Your Sheltie sees colors, but not in the same way that you do.

CAUTION

If your Sheltie is not acting normally or appears to be having problems with his eyesight, have his eyes checked right away, ideally by a board-certified veterinary ophthalmologist. Eye problems can affect behavior and may be acquired anytime throughout life. Some eye problems are inherited. Hereditary eye problems in Shelties include Collie Eye Anomaly (Sheltie Eye Syndrome) and progressive retinal atrophy.

CAUTION

Hearing problems affect behavior. Your Sheltie may have a hearing problem if he seems to be ignoring you, does not come when called, does not respond normally, or is easily frightened or confused. Hearing problems may be congenital or acquired later in life. Some hearing problems are inherited.

If you suspect your Sheltie has a hearing problem, a veterinary neurologist can test your Sheltie's hearing using a Brainstem Auditory Evoked Response (BAER) test.

Note: White-merle Shelties carry two merle genes and may be deaf in one or both ears.

Hearing

Shelties have a very keen sense of hearing, ranging from 67 Hz to 45 kHz. In comparison, human hearing range is 20 Hz to 20 kHz.

Your Sheltie's erect ears allow him to capture and increase or decrease the intensity of sound reaching his ears simply by directing an ear toward or away from the source of the sound. Your Sheltie can hear a lot of sounds that you cannot, so if he barks or becomes excited, it may be in response to something you cannot hear.

Note: Your Sheltie's ears should be erect, but the top fourth of his ear should tip and break over naturally.

Body Language

Shelties have very expressive body language, so it is easy to recognize your Sheltie's mood by his movements, body posture, and the way he carries his head, ear, and tail.

When agitated or frightened, a dog's hair may stand out straight from the body along the neck, shoulder blades, and back. This is called pilo-erection. Because Shelties carry a heavy, double coat, pilo-erection in them is not readily apparent.

Preventing and Managing Behavior Problems

The Shetland Sheepdog is, as a rule, a naturally well-adjusted and well-mannered dog. Behavior problems are not seen as commonly in Shelties as they are in many other breeds. When behavior problems develop, it is largely because owners do not spend enough time with their Shelties to adequately socialize them, or train them, or keep them mentally stimulated. Shelties are thinkers, and they love activities and challenges. They are extremely affectionate with their owners and love to spend time with them and play with them. It is only natural that such an intelligent and devoted dog would be miserable and bored when neglected, ignored, or left alone for long periods of time with nothing to do. In such cases, a Sheltie may try to find his own form of entertainment—and this can lead to trouble!

Behavior problems become reinforced when owners give their dogs mixed signals about what is acceptable behavior and what is not. This is a common problem. When dogs do not understand, they become confused and repeat the unwanted behavior. The problem becomes a vicious cycle, and everyone, dog and owner, is unhappy.

One of the most frequent mistakes people make is allowing misbehavior to continue, rather than taking immediate corrective action. If the dog does not learn immediately that the behavior is unacceptable, he will repeat it and it will soon become a habit. Unfortunately, habits are very difficult to break.

Many behavior problems are caused by fear or anxiety, and these are often caused by lack of socialization and not being introduced to new people, places, and things. Instead of trying to control or temporarily suppress a dog's undesirable behavior, it is important to identify and eliminate the cause of fear or anxiety whenever possible.

As most people are not professional dog trainers or animal therapists, it is wise for new owners to enroll in training courses together with their pets as soon as possible. Owners can sometimes inadvertently reinforce unwanted behavior and add to their dog's confusion, if a potential problem situation is not addressed immediately, consistently, and kindly. Sadly, for most dogs, undesirable behaviors are usually well established and difficult to change by the time some owners finally consult an expert.

You can prevent potential behavior problems by socializing and properly training your Sheltie (see enclosed training DVD). This is much easier, and much more successful, than trying to modify established undesirable behaviors.

If your Sheltie misbehaves, it is not because he is bad or unwilling. Shelties want to please their owners. If your Sheltie makes a mistake, it is most likely because he does not yet know exactly what you are asking of him. Teach your Sheltie in a kind, calm, and consistent manner so he can learn (see Chapter 7, "Training and Activities"). He *wants* your affection, attention, and approval. You can use this to your advantage so that training is fun and successful for both of you. *Shelties are most comfortable when they understand what is asked of them and when they know the rules and limitations. Be clear and consistent!*

PERSONALITY POINTERS

Sheltie Body Language

Mood	Friendly	Curious or Excited	Playful
Head carriage	Normal or slightly raised	Normal or slightly raised	Normal, or moving side to side, or head lowered with face raised upward
Eyes	Open, alert, gentle expression, inquisitive, direct eye contact	Open wide, alert	Open wide, direct eye contact
Ears	Alert, held high on head, or if relaxed, ears are in repose, folded lengthwise and pulled back into frill	Alert, held high on head, tilted forward	Alert, held high on head, forward, or relaxed with ears folded lengthwise and pulled back into frill
Mouth	Closed, lips tight and meeting and fitting smoothly together around mouth.	Closed or open, lips cover teeth	Closed or open, lips cover teeth
Body	Relaxed posture, weight evenly distributed on all four feet	Animated or still and observant with limbs braced, neck arched slightly forward, and body stretched so that weight is placed on front feet	Relaxed, play bow with chest lowered to ground and rump elevated, or jumping, or nudging with paws, shoulders, and hips
Tail	Wagging; when relaxed tail is carried straight down or raised in slight upward curve	Wagging and may be lifted, but not raised up over the back	Wagging, and may be relaxed or slightly lifted, depending on play activity

Apprehensive or Anxious	Fearful	Subordinate
Head turned away, slightly lowered, or pulled back slightly	Head lowered with neck muscles tensed	Head dropped low, may be turned away
Averts eyes to avoid direct eye contact, blinks	Eyes open wide, whites of eyes may be visible, dilated pupils, fixed stare	Averts eyes to avoid direct eye contact, blinks, partially closes eyes
Pulled back tightly	Pulled back tightly against skull	Pulled back against skull
Lip and nose licking, yawning, may drool	Tense, teeth visible, may drool	Lips tense and pulled back, excessive lip licking, "grinning." Grinning may be a subordinate gesture or a friendly gesture, depending on the circumstances. Shelties "grin" by pulling their lips back and displaying their teeth. Shelties may grin when they greet their owners or other dogs. Grinning is believed to be an inherited trait. Not all Shelties grin.
Tense, restless, or clinging to owner for reassurance	Tense, trembling, cowering, arched back, weight shifted to rear and poised to run	Body in submissive posture, rolls onto back and exposes underside
Tail carried lower than back but may be slightly raised	Tucked tightly between hind legs	Carried low, tucked between hind legs

Helpful Hints

Your Sheltie does not need strict disciplinary action. Shelties are sensitive to their owner's mood and very intelligent. A stern word from you, such as *no*, is sufficient to teach your Sheltie that he has done something that displeases you. Always make sure to communicate clearly with your Sheltie and avoid sending him mixed messages that may confuse him.

Six steps to behavior modification:

- Be consistent!
- Use the same word, such as *no*, to let your Sheltie know he misbehaved. Say the word once firmly and calmly. Do not shout.
- Do not reward undesirable behavior.
- Distract from the bad behavior. Then ask your Sheltie to do something he knows how to do, such as *sit* or *come*, and then praise him.
- Encourage good behavior.
- Reward good behavior only. Shelties love praise and attention!

Fears

Shelties are confident dogs and not fearful. It is their nature to be self-assured, and they are also mentally resilient. If they have an unpleasant experience, they almost always manage to adapt and adjust without being permanently emotionally traumatized. However, if a Sheltie has not been socialized, he can be fearful. Owners unintentionally reinforce their pets' fears in a number of ways. For example, one of the most common mistakes is to baby or coddle the animal and speak to him in a worried voice, or behave protectively (such as clutching the dog close to your chest) when he is shy or frightened. Owners often do this when they take their dog to the veterinarian, and then they wonder why the animal is apprehensive at the next doctor's visit! Your Sheltie should not be frightened about things that are commonplace and routinely encountered in everyday life. If you act in this manner when your Sheltie is anxious, he will think that there is indeed something to fear. Also, when you give your Sheltie attention and affection when he is frightened, you are reinforcing and rewarding his fear behavior.

Shyness and fearfulness are serious character flaws in a Shetland Sheepdog. If your Sheltie shows fear behavior, calmly distract his attention from the perceived threat (for example, you can call him to you and ask him to do something, such as *sit*) and then praise him for his good, calm, *fearless* behavior.

Barking

Shelties are barkers! This is not surprising, as many herding breeds, including the Sheltie's close relative, the Collie, are also very vocal. The Sheltie's ancestors worked outside driving and herding livestock and sounding the alert on the farm, so barking served a very important purpose. It is very possible that a tendency toward exuberant barking is an inherited trait in the Sheltie. There are individual variations and some Shelties bark more than others, but be aware that your chosen breed is a big communicator. So, if you live in an area where barking could cause problems between you and your neighbors, it may be wise to consider relocating before you acquire a Sheltie.

Most Shelties bark for a reason, such as to alert their owners of danger and intruders, but others seem to bark just for the fun of it. Sometimes the reason for barking may not be obvious, such as when the dog is responding to scents and sounds that humans cannot detect.

Some Shelties bark at everyone and everything, or bark almost incessantly. Problem barking has many causes, often stemming from lack of socialization or training, boredom, loneliness, or isolation. Many dogs bark to get attention from their owners. These dogs do not understand that excessive, incessant barking is unacceptable. Even worse, they often do not know when to *stop* barking.

Some Shelties bark excessively because they suffer from separation anxiety, fear, or even cognitive dysfunction (senile dogs especially). It is important to consult with a veterinarian who specializes in animal behavior to be certain there are no underlying health problems and to identify the cause of problem barking so it can be addressed correctly.

If your Sheltie barks excessively, teach him right away that his behavior is unacceptable. Do not make the common mistake of shouting at him to make him stop barking. This only worsens and reinforces the barking problem. From your Sheltie's perspective, your shouting means

Breed Truths

Shetland Sheepdogs are highly trainable and eager to please. Males and females are equally intelligent, although some females may be more energetic and dynamic than males. Shelties are amiable with other dogs and avoid fights. Males may be housed together peacefully, and many have been known to join the females in playing "nanny" to small puppies.

29

CAUTION

We often try to "fix" many of our behavior problems with medications. We do this for ourselves and for our children, and we now do it for our pets. But preventing behavior problems is better and easier than treating them. You can prevent behavior problems by giving your Sheltie the time and attention he needs and deserves, and through early, positive socialization and training. Shelties are naturally confident dogs. If your Sheltie is apprehensive or fearful, identify the cause and act in a calm, matter-of-fact manner to reassure him. *Do not give your Sheltie sedatives to calm him, unless your veterinarian specifically prescribes them.*

Approximately 15 percent of Shetland Sheepdogs in the United States carry a genetic mutation (called the MDR1 gene deletion) that makes them overly sensitive to more than 20 kinds of medications, including some kinds of sedatives. These drugs can cause health problems or even death in Shelties that have this gene mutation. Fortunately, Shelties can be tested for this gene (see Chapter 6, "Health and Nutrition").

Medications for behavioral modification should be considered only as a last resort for difficult cases in which the dog does not respond to training, socialization, and other behavioral modification methods.

you are joining in the excitement and cacophony, so there must be a reason to bark! Instead, distract him from the unwanted behavior. Call him to you and ask him to *sit*. Then, reward him for being calm and *quiet*. Make sure your Sheltie understands that he is being rewarded for *not* barking and for being quiet. If you call him and reward him immediately when he barks, he will think he is being rewarded for barking. This is why it is very important to first distract him by asking him to do something other than bark. Your Sheltie must clearly understand that the reward is for obeying and being calm and quiet, and that it is *not* for barking.

Sometimes you can anticipate that your dog will bark before he does it. In these situations, distract him *before* he barks. Call him to you, ask him to sit or lie down, and then praise him. The more often you can prevent the bad habit, the faster you can modify your Sheltie's behavior. There are additional training methods that can be successful in correcting problem barking (see Chapter 10, "Special Considerations").

If you can identify the cause or stimulus for the unwanted barking and if there is a way to eliminate it, then do so. For example, if your Sheltie barks at a specific item, such as a yard sprinkler, then bring him inside while the sprinklers run. Of course, if your Sheltie barks for a good reason, such as smoke in the house, or an attempted burglary, you will naturally praise and reward him for his courageous behavior!

Chewing

Puppies investigate with their mouths and have a natural urge to chew, especially while their puppy teeth, and later their adult teeth, are erupting. Dogs love to chew! All dogs should be given safe, inde-structible chew toys for their well-being and entertainment.

You can prevent your Sheltie from chewing on the wrong things if you

Helpful Hints

Teach your Sheltie that he can chew only on the safe chew toys that you give him. Do not give your puppy something inappropriate to chew, such as an old shoe, because your Sheltie will think that means *all* shoes are good to chew. Your Sheltie does not know the difference between an old shoe and a brand new one!

- give your Sheltie lots of interesting, safe, chew toys;
- supervise your puppy's chewing activities at all times;
- make sure all valuables (furniture, shoes, books) and harmful items (children's toys, pieces of plastic, electrical cords, bones) are out of your puppy's reach;
- prevent boredom and give your Sheltie lots of attention, activities, and exercise, and take him on frequent walks and outings.

If your Sheltie chews on something he should not, simply distract him by offering him one of his own chew toys. Do not chase him to take the object away. He might think you are playing a game.

Destructive chewing is different from regular chewing. Dogs chew because they naturally enjoy it, and they are happy to chew on their assigned chew toys. Continual destructive chewing is the result of a lack of appropriate environmental enrichment and interesting chew toys, boredom, noise phobias, frustration, confinement anxiety, separation anxiety, or obsessive compulsive disorders.

Breed Truths

While researching the MDR-1 gene, a gene mutation found in Shelties and other herding breeds, scientists discovered, through DNA analysis, that the mutation traced back to a dog that lived in Great Britain in the 1800s. They also learned that this dog is the ancestor of at least nine different modern-day breeds, including the Collie and Shetland Sheepdog.

Play Biting

It is natural for dogs to explore and play with their mouths. Shelties may lightly nip each other when they play, but your Sheltie should learn from the day you acquire him, that biting humans, even playfully, is not allowed. Puppies that are allowed to bite eventually grow into adult dogs—that still bite. Puppy teeth are surprisingly sharp weapons that can inflict damage, especially to children. Adult canine teeth can do even more harm, even if it is unintentional and meant to be "in play."

One of the ways your Sheltie may try to attract your attention is by mouthing your hands, or grabbing at the cuffs of your sleeves or the bottom of your pants. If you allow him to do this, it can become an undesirable habit, and you may end up with scratches on your hands and holes in your clothing. Or worse, you may trip over your Sheltie and one or both of you may be injured while he is wandering between your legs, pulling at the hems of your slacks. When your Sheltie engages in any unwanted behavior, do not reward him with your attention or by petting him. Instead, correct him immediately, but kindly. For example, if he nips at you when

you are playing, say "Ouch!" and then "No!" Then give him a chew toy to redirect his actions and modify his behavior. He will quickly learn that chew toys are to chew and bite, but fingers and hands are not.

Never hit, swat, strike, shake, or physically punish your Shetland Sheepdog.

Separation Anxiety

Separation anxiety cases make up 19 percent of canine problem-behavior cases referred to veterinary behavior specialists. Dogs suffering from separation anxiety are overly attached (hyperattached) to their owners and become anxious when their owners are not within their sight or leave home without them. These animals usually begin to bark and whine, destroy objects, and sometimes soil in the house almost immediately after the owner leaves. In some cases the dogs may try to escape their confinement, drool, pant, pace, vomit, or lick or chew themselves. They may develop diarrhea, become depressed, and refuse to eat.

Fun Facts

Studies are under way to detect the genes responsible for certain behavioral traits. Researchers expect to soon unveil the identities of the genes that control behaviors typically observed in Shetland Sheepdogs, such as temperament, herding ability, trainability, and loyalty.

Shelties thrive on the companionship of their human family members. Shelties should never be left alone or ignored for long periods of time, especially on a continual basis, or they may suffer from separation anxiety. If a problem develops, the following tips may be helpful:

- Develop a predictable daily routine, so your Sheltie knows what to expect and when.
- Offer rewards (food treats, interesting toys, praise, games) for good, calm behavior.
- Ignore undesirable behavior.
- Set up a special area for your Sheltie and give him some chew toys, food rewards, and even an old piece of your clothing (for scent). Leave the area for a short time period and return with a reward for calm, good behavior. Gradually extend the time away before returning with a reward.
- Counterconditioning can be helpful. For example, if certain departure cues, such as picking up your car keys or putting on your coat, make your Sheltie anxious, try doing these actions without leaving and then reward your Sheltie for good behavior.
- Leave the house when your Sheltie is calm, not excited, or when he is asleep or distracted with a toy or activity.
- Be matter-of-fact and calm about leaving the house.
- When you return, be calm and simply ask your Sheltie to sit or lie down. Then, reward him only when he is calm.

Chapter Three

How to Choose a Shetland Sheepdog

The first steps to acquiring a healthy Shetland Sheepdog are to *learn as much as possible about the breed, be absolutely sure a Sheltie is the right dog for you, and then find a reputable Sheltie source.*

Your Sheltie may live 15 years or more. During that time he will be a devoted companion and a big part of your life. You are making a long-term commitment to your new canine friend. It must be a perfect match!

Considerations

Is a Shetland Sheepdog the Best Dog for You?

Shetland Sheepdogs are endearing, versatile, bright, beautiful, and loyal—but that doesn't necessarily mean that a Sheltie is the best dog for you. It's important that your lifestyle is also compatible with dog ownership and that your Sheltie's personality complements your own. Timing has to be right, too. Is this a good time in your life for you to acquire a new pet? Do you have the time and resources to provide a Sheltie with the care, training, nutrition, regular grooming, and close companionship that he deserves? Take the test!

1. Do you enjoy the company of a dog that bonds closely with you, loves to play and travel, and wants to be part of all of your family activities?
2. Are you looking for a dog that is sensitive, responsive, sweet, gentle, affectionate, loyal, and highly trainable?
3. Do you have time to exercise your Sheltie every day?
4. Will you feed your Sheltie a high-quality diet according to his age, condition, activity level, and nutritional needs?
5. Do you enjoy dog training, and would you like to participate in a variety of dog events?
6. Do you enjoy dog grooming, and do you have the time to do it? Can you live with a long-haired dog that sheds periodically? (If you have allergies to animal hair and dander, consult with your physician before obtaining any dog.)

7. Do you live in an area where barking would not disturb your neighbors? Shelties can be barkers!

8. Can you provide your Sheltie with routine and emergency health care? Do you have a veterinarian for him?

9. Are you able and prepared to care for a dog that could live 15 years or longer? Will you set aside funds and make arrangements for your Sheltie's care in case something happens to you and you can no longer look after him?

10. Have you compared Shetland Sheepdogs with other breeds? Do you still think a Sheltie is the best match for you?

If you answered "yes" to these questions, then you just might be ready to join the ranks of thousands of people worldwide who have owned and loved a Sheltie!

Ideally, it is helpful to attend some dog shows and observe as many Shelties as you can to see firsthand all the activities a Sheltie can do, how Shelties normally behave, and what a well-bred Sheltie looks like. When you have the opportunity to see how wonderful Shelties are in person and in action, you can judge for yourself which dogs appeal to you the most. Dog shows are a great place to meet fellow Sheltie enthusiasts, exhibitors, trainers, and breeders. Word of mouth at a dog show is often a good way to find a trustworthy Sheltie source. If you buy a show catalog, you can match the people to their dogs. This may ultimately lead you to the breeder of your future Sheltie. You can find show schedules and locations on the American Kennel Club website (*www.akc.org*).

Breed Truths

Still a Baby!

Shetland Sheepdog puppies are small and need time to develop and grow. They should not leave the breeder's home before 8 weeks of age. Some breeders will not place puppies until they are at least 12 to 16 weeks old.

Note: It is against the law in many states to sell a puppy before it is 8 weeks old.

Sheltie Choices

Every Sheltie is a unique individual. When choosing a Shetland Sheepdog, the most important things to consider are the Sheltie's health, personality, and temperament. The age, sex, color, and markings of your Sheltie are secondary.

Puppy, Adolescent, or Adult?

Do you want a puppy, an adolescent, or an adult Shetland Sheepdog? It can be a tough decision. Sheltie puppies are irresistibly cute, but puppies are puppies for only a few months. Owning a puppy means that you will have to spend a lot of time at home. Your puppy will need frequent meals, continual

care, and constant supervision. He will need to be socialized, housetrained, leash trained, crate and travel trained, and trained to be groomed. That's a lot of training—and time! For some people, a well-mannered adolescent or adult Sheltie is a better choice.

Sometimes breeders have adolescent or young-adult dogs available for the right family. These Shelties may have been initially retained for exhibiting or breeding, but may not have turned out as the breeder had hoped. For example, they may have grown slightly taller than the breed standard allows. This doesn't stop these Shelties from being wonderful companions. They might not win in the show ring, but they easily win over hearts! Rarely, you may find older Shelties available, such as retired breeders or even retired champions. These adults are highly trained, well socialized, and well mannered. They are a true pleasure for a new owner, who can bypass the challenges of puppyhood and training and focus on simply enjoying a new friend.

Breed Truths

Puppy Love for Life

Shetland Sheepdogs were bred to be companions and working partners. These characteristics are deeply ingrained in today's Sheltie. Shelties want to spend every moment possible with their human families. It is not unusual for a Sheltie to bond especially closely with one specific family member. The love at first sight that you experience when you first meet your Sheltie puppy is a love that will last a lifetime.

Shelties are highly adaptable dogs. They adapt to almost all lifestyles, from city and apartment living to country life on the farm. They do not require a lot of space, as long as they have daily exercise.

Shelties are friendly, but it is their nature to be reserved with strangers. Understandably, older Shelties may take a little while to become acquainted and bond with a new family. The breeder will probably ask you to give the adoption a trial period, just to be sure your new Sheltie adapts successfully to his new family and new environment.

Fun Facts

In one survey of 140 breeds, Shelties ranked sixth for obedience and working intelligence. Shelties also rank high on the list of the top 10 breeds earning the largest number of obedience titles.

Shetland Sheepdog breeders invest a lot of time, effort, training, and money in their animals. The older an animal is, the greater the investment, so an adult Sheltie may cost more than a puppy.

The price you pay for your Sheltie is insignificant compared with what you will invest in time, training, feeding, grooming, supplies, toys, housing, and veterinary care during his long lifetime. Make sure you have time for a Shetland Sheepdog and can afford one, not just now, but also in the many years to come.

COMPATIBILITY Is a Shetland Sheepdog the Best Breed for You?

ENERGY LEVEL	● ● ● ●
PERSONAL ATTENTION TIME REQUIREMENT	● ● ● ●
EXERCISE REQUIREMENT	● ● ● ●
PLAYFULNESS	● ● ● ●
AFFECTION LEVEL	● ● ● ● ●
FRIENDLINESS TOWARD OTHER PETS	● ● ● ● ●
FRIENDLINESS TOWARD STRANGERS	● ● ●
FRIENDLINESS TOWARD CHILDREN	● ● ● ●
EASE OF TRAINING	● ● ● ● ●
GROOMING REQUIREMENTS	● ● ● ● ●
SPACE REQUIREMENTS	● ● ●
OK FOR BEGINNERS	● ● ● ●

5 Dots = Highest rating on scale

Personality

A Sheltie's best quality is its winning personality. Shelties are endearing, charming, clever, playful, and enthusiastic. They are keenly attached, attuned, and *responsive* to their owners—and they expect their owners to respond to them as well. Shelties are *sensitive*, kind dogs. They respond quickly to words, gestures, facial expressions, and voice intonations. If you are sad, your Sheltie will know and try to comfort you. If you are happy, your Sheltie will share in your joy. If you want to go somewhere or do something, your Sheltie will be the first to join you in the adventure. When you are too busy to play, your Sheltie will be happy just to be close to you. When you sit at your desk, your Sheltie may lie down beside your chair to take a nap. He won't be a nuisance or be in the way, but don't be surprised if he places his foot on top of yours to make sure you are there and to know when you get up to leave.

Everything a Shetland Sheepdog experiences in his life can affect his personality and behavior. The most critical and formative stage of his behavioral development is from 3 to 12 weeks of age. A Shetland Sheepdog's personality is already well established by the time he is 8 to 12 weeks old. Bonding, socialization, and handling during a Shetland Sheepdog's formative stages are extremely important. Frequent handling in a kind and gentle manner from birth, exposure to various sights and sounds in a non-frightening and reassuring way, meeting new people and animals, exploring new places, and investigating new and interesting toys are all part of the socialization process. A well-socialized Shetland Sheepdog is confident, happy, and openly communicative with its human friends.

Male or Female

Male Shetland Sheepdogs are generally larger than females, carry a heavier coat, and are clearly masculine in appearance. Males are often credited with being calmer and more even-tempered than females. The truth is, every Shetland Sheepdog is different. Although there are certain characteristics and behaviors set in the breed, every Sheltie is an individual with a unique personality. Traits and temperament are influenced by numerous factors. Socialization, past experiences, genetics, and environment all play a role in the formation of a Shetland Sheepdog's character. Whether you choose a male or a female, the choice is simply a matter of personal preference. You will be delighted either way!

Companion or Competition Sheltie?

All Shetland Sheepdogs are, first and foremost, companions. They bond closely with their owners and give them constant companionship. So when a breeder asks you if you are looking for a companion or competition or show dog, the question might seem odd at first. What the breeder really wants to know is, in addition to having a Sheltie to love as a family member, do you have any other expectations of your pet? Do you plan to participate in competitive events, in which the dog is judged on performance (such as agility, herding, obedience, tracking)? Or do you want to exhibit your Sheltie in conformation, where the dog is judged on beauty and movement? Perhaps you own a ranch and need a true working and herding dog. Or is your Sheltie destined to be strictly a family companion? The answer to these questions will help you and the breeder select the Sheltie that is the best match for you.

All Shetland Sheepdogs are companions, but not all Shetland Sheepdogs are performance and show dogs. A companion Shetland Sheepdog is an affectionate, devoted member of the family. Shetland Sheepdogs that are show dogs are also very devoted companions, but they must also closely adhere to the breed standard regarding conformation, height, character, gait, and color. A performance Sheltie has to demonstrate the abilities to compete and the desire and instinct to work for which the breed has been carefully selected. The differences between a show and/or performance Shetland Sheepdog and a companion Shetland Sheepdog are obvious to the trained eye of a breeder, judge, handler, trainer, or other dog experts, but may not be readily apparent to the general public.

If you have decided that you want a dog for competition and/or exhibition, be prepared to pay more for him than you would pay for a companion pet. Also, keep in mind that although the parents may be title winners and champions, there is no guarantee that their offspring will achieve the same success.

Helpful Hints

Show dog or show-off?

Just because the puppies' parents are champions doesn't mean the puppies will also be champions. No one can predict with certainty that a puppy will become a title winner, although experienced breeders can detect puppies with potential. Puppies constantly change as they develop, grow, and mature. The true test of a show or performance prospect is his ability to win among the top competitors in the ring.

Whether in the show ring or in the neighborhood, Shetland Sheepdogs are happiest when they are pleasing their owners.

Color

Accepted colors for the Shetland Sheepdog are sable, tricolor (black with white and tan markings), bi-black (black with white markings), blue-merle (blue-merle with white and tan markings), and bi-blue (blue-merle with white markings). These have been described in detail (see Chapter 1, "All About Shetland Sheepdogs").

White markings may be present on the face, collar, feet, legs, and tip of the tail. In tricolors and blue-merles, tan markings are present on the cheeks, above the eyes, and often on the legs. Tan markings are absent on bi-blacks

(black and white) and bi-blues (blue-merle and white). Lack of white markings on the face or collar is not a fault.

Noses are black, and eyes should be dark (blue-merles and bi-blues may have blue in one or both eyes).

Note: Blue eyes are not visually defective. Just like people, Shetland Sheepdogs with blue eyes can see as well as Shetland Sheepdogs with brown eyes.

Age and Longevity

With loving care, exercise, and good nutrition, Shetland Sheepdogs can live well into their teens. Take your time and choose your new companion very carefully. You will be spending many years together!

Finding a Breeder

A knowledgeable, dedicated Shetland Sheepdog breeder is the best and most reliable source for a healthy, well-socialized Sheltie. Breeding and raising high-quality Shetland Sheepdogs is rewarding, but hard work. It is time consuming, demanding, and challenging. There are many people who call themselves "dog breeders," but that doesn't mean that they are reputable, or that they have healthy, well-socialized dogs. Not all "dog breeders" have a dog's best interests at heart. Some people breed dogs for money, cutting corners on care and nutrition and hoping to profit from the breed's popularity. Other people are well-intentioned newcomers who simply do not know what they are doing. Whether breeding dogs indiscriminately or breeding

FYI: Puppy Mills

Do not buy a Shetland Sheepdog that originates from a puppy mill! Puppy mills (also called "puppy farms") are dog-breeding operations that raise dogs in large quantities for mass marketing, without regard for the animals' well-being, genetics, quality, or health. The puppies are often raised in cramped, dirty facilities, with inadequate nutrition and little human contact. They are often afflicted with health and genetic problems.

dogs ignorantly, these kinds of "dog breeders" are the ones to avoid.

Good Shetland Sheepdog breeders have years of experience and a solid understanding of the breed. They know the family lines behind their dogs in detail. They show and compete with their Shelties and screen them for health problems. These breeders invest the necessary *time* and *money* to provide their animals with the love, attention, training, grooming, housing, exercise, nutrition, and health care they need. They do not profit from dog sales, because their investment is so great. In fact, when done correctly, dog breeding is a negative cash flow hobby. It is a labor of love. Dedicated breeders raise Shelties to improve the breed's beauty, health, and genetics with each new generation. They give their Shelties the very best and it shows. *These* are the people you want to contact for your new Sheltie!

CAUTION

Beware of sellers who advertise puppies but do not thoroughly interview you, or who try to pressure you into a sale, or who are more interested in receiving your payment than they are in the type of home you can provide their puppies. These individuals do not have the puppy's best interest at heart—or yours. They may be puppy mills or they may be scams.

One excellent source for finding reputable, respected Shetland Sheepdog breeders is the American Kennel Club (*www.akc.org*). The AKC website has a breeder-referral site (*www.akc.org/breederinfo/breeder_search.cfm*) and a breeder classified-listings section (*www.akc.org/classified/search/index.cfm*). The AKC website gives information on local Shetland Sheepdog specialty clubs and show events. Another great source for finding a good Sheltie breeder is the national parent club: the American Shetland Sheepdog Association (*www.assa.org*). The ASSA website provides breeder referrals, a list of rescue groups, and detailed information on the Shetland Sheepdog Breed Standard, as well as show information and fun activities you can do with your Sheltie.

One fun way to find Shetland Sheepdog breeders is to attend dog shows or join a dog club. It is a perfect way to meet other Sheltie enthusiasts, as well as trainers, handlers, judges, and groomers who can help you find a dedicated breeder.

CAUTION

Don't Be an "Impulse Buyer" or "Sympathy Buyer"

It is easy to fall for the charm of the first Shetland Sheepdog you find, but that captivating creature may not be the best match for you. Take time to visit as many breeders and look at as many puppies as possible before you make your final choice. The Shetland Sheepdog you select should be healthy, well socialized, and well bred. Do not buy a Shetland Sheepdog puppy that is reclusive, fearful, or nervous. Do not buy a Sheltie puppy that is seriously undersized (runt), weak, or shows even the slightest signs of illness. It is normal to feel sorry for these animals, but these are indicators that something is seriously wrong. It is the breeder's responsibility to take care of these problems. Don't let sympathy distract your focus from a confident, healthy puppy. Fearful, sick puppies can mean serious medical or behavioral problems now and in the future, as well as significant medical expenses and possible heartbreak later on. Use your head and consider only the most healthy, confident, outgoing puppies. Then use your heart for your final selection among them.

Dedicated Breeders

When you find a reputable Shetland Sheepdog breeder, you might have to wait for the right puppy or dog. Many top breeders have a wait list for dogs. If you have special preferences as to your Sheltie's sex, color, or age, then it may take even longer to find your ideal companion. Keep in mind that your Sheltie's health, temperament, and personality are more important than its sex, color, or markings.

You will have a lot of questions for breeders as you search for your perfect companion. The breeders will have plenty of questions for you, too, because they truly care about their dogs' future and well-being. Their top priority is placing their dogs with the right person, in an ideal home environment.

Here are some questions you may want to ask the breeder:

1. How long has the breeder been raising and showing Shetland Sheepdogs?
2. Is the breeder a member in good standing with the American Shetland Sheepdog Association?
3. What are the details of the breeder's health guarantee, and which heritable diseases are screened?
4. Does the breeder have a sales contract?
5. Does the breeder require a spay/neuter agreement?

6. Does the breeder have registration documents, pedigrees, photos, health certifications, and medical records available to review? These include vaccine history, an eye examination report provided by a board-certified veterinary ophthalmologist, and DNA test results.
7. Does the breeder provide a health guarantee of 48 to 72 hours to give you time to have the puppy examined and declared healthy by your veterinarian?
8. Will the breeder take the dog back, or help you find him a home, if something happens and you are no longer able to take care of him?

Choosing a Shetland Sheepdog Puppy

You have decided a Shetland Sheepdog is the right dog for you, and you have found some reputable Shetland Sheepdog sources. Now comes the fun part—and the most difficult part: choosing a Shetland Sheepdog that is perfect for you! *Take your time and use good judgment* as you select your ideal canine companion.

Whenever possible, once you have located a breeder, call and ask for an appointment to meet the breeder and ask to see the available puppies and their parents, in person.

BE PREPARED! A Dozen Questions to Ask About the Puppies

1. Are the pups registered with a recognized kennel club, such as the American Kennel Club?
2. How old are the pups, and at what age were they weaned?
3. Have the pups been examined by a veterinarian? If so, have they been vaccinated? With which vaccinations? What is the veterinarian's recommended vaccine schedule?
4. Do the pups have any special health certifications from veterinary specialists, such as eye examinations? (See Chapter 6, "Health and Nutrition," for information about Optigen DNA testing and the Canine Eye Registration Foundation.)
5. Have the pups been tested or treated for internal and external parasites?
6. Are there any known health problems in the puppy's family lines?
7. What kind of socialization and training have the pups received so far?
8. What kind of food do the pups eat? How much and how often do they eat?
9. Ask to see the parents and littermates of the pup and the environment where the puppies are raised.
10. Will the breeder take the dog back, or help you find him a home, if something unexpected happens that makes you unable to care for him?
11. How many puppies were in the litter? What colors and sexes are available?
12. What additional information does the breeder think is important for you to know about the puppies? Can you contact the breeder in the future if you have additional questions?

When you arrive at the breeder's, take note of the animals' home environment, including cleanliness, housing, and play areas. Observe the puppies closely. Are they healthy, happy, alert, active, and playful? Hiding, trembling, growling, or nipping in fear are completely unacceptable Shetland Sheepdog behaviors. Any puppy that responds to you in this manner should be immediately eliminated from your canine companion candidate list.

Look for the puppy with correct Sheltie temperament. That will be the puppy that is most confident, responsive, and interested, yet reserved. This puppy may continue his activities away from you, but he will still keep a watch on you. Be patient. Shelties prefer to make the first move to investigate and initiate a friendship. It may take a few minutes before he comes up to you—in his own time. Shelties don't give their hearts away instantly. You will first have to earn your puppy's trust before you can win his friendship.

While you are holding your favorite Shetland Sheepdog puppy, check the eyes, ears, nose, mouth, gums, teeth, skin, and coat. The eyes should be clear and bright. The ears should be clean. Normal gums are bright pink in color. In older puppies, some of the adult teeth may be coming in and replacing the baby (deciduous) teeth. Wherever adult teeth have erupted, the baby teeth

BE PREPARED! A Dozen Questions the Breeder Will Ask You

1. Why do you want a Shetland Sheepdog? What do you want or expect from your Sheltie?
2. Do you have experience with Shetland Sheepdogs? Have you previously owned a Sheltie?
3. Do you have the time and finances to properly care for a Shetland Sheepdog now and in the long-range future?
4. What kind of home can you provide?
5. Do you have other pets or children in the home? If so, what type of pets and how old are the children?
6. Do you enjoy grooming, and do you have time to do it? If not, are you able to hire a groomer on a regular basis?
7. Do you have a fenced-in yard, patio, or safe enclosure for a Sheltie?
8. How many hours a day are you home? Do you have time to care for your Shetland Sheepdog, including playtime and daily walks?
9. Can you provide the name and phone number of your veterinarian for a reference?
10. Can the breeder meet your family members who will be living with the Sheltie?
11. Do you plan to take your Sheltie with you on trips and vacations?
12. Do you promise to contact the breeder in the event that you are no longer able to keep or care for your Sheltie?

should have fallen out. If the baby teeth do not come out when the adult teeth grow in, there will be too many teeth in the mouth and dental problems will result. Retained deciduous teeth must be extracted.

Check the skin to be sure it is free of parasites, flakiness, lumps, bumps, and sores. The coat should be in good condition and well groomed, free of knots and mats. Look under the tail to be sure the area is clean and that there are no signs of blood, diarrhea, or parasites.

Ask to see your puppy's littermates and parents. The mother is usually available to see, but do not be surprised if you cannot see the father. The stud dog may belong to another breeder and live far away, out of state, or even out of the country.

When you observe the personalities, behaviors, and appearances of the parents

Helpful Hints

Ouch! Those Teeth Are Sharp!

Puppies must learn not to use their mouths in play with humans. Puppies can get excited and nip, especially during play or while chasing. If your Sheltie nips, say "No" very firmly and distract him with a toy. Shelties are sensitive dogs. They need only a firm voice reprimand (see Chapter 7, "Training and Activities"). *Never shout at your Sheltie, and never hit, strike, or shake him.*

PERSONALITY POINTERS

Shetland Sheepdog Personality

Normal Shetland Sheepdog	Shetland Sheepdog Problem Behavior
• Personality	• Fearful
• Sensitive and sensible	• Shy
• Responsive	• Reclusive
• Playful	• Runs, hides, or cowers when approached
• Reserved	
• Inquisitive	• Growls without provocation
• Affectionate	• Aggressive
• Sweet	• Nips with intent to harm
• Acquiescent	• Fear-biter
• Willing	• Incompatible with littermates
• Eager to please	• Struggles to escape when picked up
• Good-natured	• Yelps or protests when held
• Compatible with littermates	• Does not enjoy human company
• Interested in new sights and sounds, and investigates	• Does not enjoy attention
	• Does not want to be petted
• Watchful of strangers, but friendly after it has had time to become acquainted	• Is not eager to please
• Loves attention from owner	

and the littermates, you have a better idea of how your chosen Sheltie might look and behave as an adult. Of course, the way you raise and handle your puppy, and his various experiences, have a big influence on his character development.

Plan to spend lots of time with your Sheltie. The more time you spend socializing and training your puppy, the closer he will bond to you and the more confident and happy he will be as an adult.

Health Records, Kennel Club Registration, and Pedigree

Before making a final decision and completing the sale, be sure the puppy's health records, kennel club registration papers, pedigree, and other documents are in order and available.

Health Record Your puppy should have a health certificate signed by a veterinarian saying the puppy has been examined within the past 10 days and is in good health and able to travel to his new home. Dates of vaccinations, treatments, and medications should be noted on the health certificate or medical record. You and your veterinarian will need this information to set up a preventive health care program for your new Shetland Sheepdog.

CHECKLIST

Is the Puppy Healthy?

✔ **Overall impression:** Healthy, clean, alert, active, very good body condition, attractive coat, normal gait and movement

✔ **Eyes:** Bright, clear, free of discharge

✔ **Ears:** Clean, free of dirt, discharge, and wax buildup; no bad odor; no head-shaking; no scratching at the ears

✔ **Nose:** Clean, no signs of discharge

✔ **Mouth:** Gums pink, teeth correctly aligned; when teeth are erupting the gums may be temporarily swollen and sore; no duplicate teeth (deciduous and adult of the same type)

✔ **Skin and coat:** Healthy skin; dense, well-groomed coat free of knots, mats, sores, and parasites

✔ **Body condition:** Body a little plump, not thin; should not have a grossly distended belly

✔ **Movement:** Normal gait for a puppy, bouncy and prancing.

BE PREPARED! What Will My Dog Cost Me?

The American Veterinary Medical Association says that the average pet owner spends about $350 annually on veterinary care for each dog owned. Shelties are hardy, resilient dogs, but it is wise to set funds aside for an emergency and to be realistic about what Sheltie ownership can cost. The following is a guideline of the minimum amount Sheltie ownership costs per year:

Food: Shelties do not eat much, but they require top-quality nutrition (see Chapter 6, "Health and Nutrition"). Dog food prices vary according to region and quality, and prices continue to rise. Prescription diets are more expensive. $400 to $700

Veterinary care: Depends on the age, sex, health, and lifestyle of the dog. Veterinary fees vary; specialists' fees are higher. Laboratory tests, surgery, dental care, or medical emergency can cost hundreds to thousands of dollars. Estimate is for a healthy dog requiring only an annual examination, routine laboratory tests, and vaccinations. $500

Note: The American Kennel Club offers a health insurance program.

Accessories: The basics (crate, exercise pen, collar, leash, bed, dishes, toys, grooming supplies). $350

Boarding facility or pet sitter: $20 to $35 daily

Travel: Additional fee for hotels that accept dogs. $15 to $25 per day plus deposit

Liability insurance: Varies according to insurance company. $100

License: Varies according to county and state; licenses for neutered dogs are discounted. $15 to $35

Kennel Club Registration When you purchase your Shetland Sheepdog, make sure that he has been registered with a *recognized* kennel club, such as the American Kennel Club. The registration is an official document issued by a recognized kennel club. It is proof that your dog is a purebred Shetland Sheepdog. The registration also opens the door to the pleasures of competing in many official dog activities. Without registration papers, there is no proof of your Sheltie's parentage or breed and your dog cannot participate in many kennel club events.

Reputable breeders register their litters. Be wary of any breeder who cannot provide you with proof of litter registration. Official registration is not the same as a pedigree. The kennel club issues the registration. Anyone can write up a pedigree.

If the kennel club in which your Shetland Sheepdog is registered is not the American Kennel Club, check into the kennel club's authenticity before you purchase your Shetland Sheepdog. The American Kennel Club was established in 1884 and is world renowned. Unfortunately, some groups

CHECKLIST

Paperwork

✔ Health guarantee from the breeder and other contractual information such as spay/neuter agreements, return and refund policies, sales contract

✔ Health certificate from a veterinarian verifying that the puppy was examined and is healthy

✔ Medical record listing all vaccines and treatments the animal has received and the dates they were administered

✔ Microchip identification number and documentation, including forms for the dog's new owner to register with the microchip database

✔ Kennel club registration application form or transfer of ownership, signed by the breeder, owner, and co-owner when indicated. Check whether your puppy has limited registration or full registration.

✔ Pedigree listing the names, titles, and other information about the dog's parents, grandparents, and great-grandparents

✔ Additional documents, such as eye certifications or DNA test results (such as for MDR1 gene, eye disorders, or DNA profiling)

✔ Dog license and proof of rabies vaccination, when applicable

✔ Written care instructions from the breeder, including feeding instructions and recommended diet, veterinarian, grooming parlor, obedience class, dog club

✔ Sales receipt

claiming to be "official kennel clubs" are little more than companies that charge you money to print out a copy of your dog's pedigree.

Registration Application When you purchase your Shetland Sheepdog, the breeder will give you a registration application. If the dog has already been named and registered, the breeder will sign the back of the registration form, indicating that ownership has been transferred to you. The registration application lists the breeder, the litter registration number, the litter birth date, and the names and registration numbers of your puppy's parents. Whoever registers the dog has the right to name it; however, many breeders request that their kennel name be included as part of the dog's full registered name.

If you are submitting the registration application form, choose a name for your Shetland Sheepdog and submit the application form to the kennel club address on the back of the form along with the indicated registration fee. The American Kennel Club allows you to register online (*www.AKC.org*). You will then receive a certificate of registration from the kennel club, showing the dog's official name and you as the new owner.

FYI: The National Parent Club

The American Shetland Sheepdog Association (*www.assa.org*) is an excellent source of information for Sheltie owners. It provides information on the breed, the detailed breed standard, show information, educational opportunities, lists of activities to do with your Sheltie, ethics, guidelines, articles, breeder referrals, rescue contacts, membership information, and much more.

If your Shetland Sheepdog was born in the United States, the breeder will decide whether he receives a full registration or a limited registration.

Full Registration A full registration is printed on a white piece of paper with a purple border. It lists the breeder, the owner, the registered name and number of the dog, and its birth date, breed, color, and sex. The dog's parents and their titles or certifications are also indicated. Full registration allows for participation in AKC competitions and events, as well as the ability to register future offspring of the animal with the AKC.

Limited Registration A limited registration contains the same information as a full registration certificate and looks the same except the border is orange. Dogs with limited registration cannot be used for breeding purposes. If they produce puppies, their puppies cannot be registered with the AKC. Only the breeder, not the owner, can change an animal's status from limited to full registration.

Pedigree A pedigree is a chart showing the dog's family tree. Breeders often prepare pedigrees for buyers, listing the parents, grandparents, and great-grandparents of the puppy for sale. A pedigree from the breeder is not an official document and does not guarantee that the dog is registered with a recognized kennel club. However, if you do not have a pedigree, and your Shetland Sheepdog is registered with the AKC, you can order a detailed pedigree, suitable for framing, directly from the AKC. The AKC pedigree lists the names, registration numbers, coat colors, and certain awards and certifications of your Shetland Sheepdog's family.

Shetland Sheepdog Rescue

It is hard to imagine that any Shetland Sheepdog could end up homeless, neglected, or unwanted.

There are many reasons why a Shetland Sheepdog may lose his home. Some of the most common reasons people list for relinquishing or abandoning their animals include moving; not enough time, space, or money; personal issues (divorce, changing jobs, new baby, illness, death in the family);

FYI: PAL/ILP

The Purebred Alternative Listing/Indefinite Listing Privilege (PAL/ILP) is a program offered by the American Kennel Club. It allows registration of dogs from undocumented backgrounds (such as rescue dogs) so that they can participate in AKC events such as agility, herding, obedience, rally, tracking, and junior showmanship. To apply for registration, the owner must provide a veterinary certificate saying the dog has been spayed or neutered, two recent color photographs (front of face and side of body), and an application fee of $35. More information can be found at *www.akc.org*.

excessive barking; or the animal is sick and the owner cannot afford veterinary care.

Whatever the reason for relinquishment, the result is tragic. The loyal Shetland Sheepdog that thrives on human companionship no longer has a family or home.

A rescue Shetland Sheepdog may be well behaved and of sound temperament. Or, he may have behavior problems, especially if he was neglected and did not receive adequate socialization or training.

If you are up to the challenge of rescuing a Shetland Sheepdog, the experience can be rewarding beyond words. Contact the American Shetland Sheepdog Association (*www.assa.org*).

All rescue Shelties are examined by a veterinarian, vaccinated, and spayed (ovariohysterectomy) or neutered (castration). Many go to temporary foster homes where they are evaluated and assessed so they can be placed in a permanent home that is right for them. There is a nominal adoption fee. Shetland Sheepdogs that are older or that have health problems are usually more expensive to care for, but they give love and friendship that money cannot buy.

When rescue Shelties join their new family, their AKC registration papers (if they have any) do not go with them. However, the new owners can apply for a Purebred Alternative Listing/Indefinite Listing Privilege (PAL/ILP) number through the AKC. This allows them to participate in AKC companion and performance events.

If you cannot rescue a Sheltie at this time, there are lots of other ways you can help these unfortunate animals find loving homes, including donating and volunteering. The rescue organizations will be grateful for your help and the Shelties will be, too!

Chapter Four

Caring for a Shetland Sheepdog Puppy

You have found your perfect Sheltie puppy! Now it is time to bring him home and make him feel loved, safe, and comfortable in his new surroundings. Your puppy will bond to you closely and adapt more quickly to his new environment if you are sensitive to his emotions and needs. Things will also go more smoothly for both of you if everything is prepared and ready *before* you bring your Sheltie home.

Puppy Proofing

Sheltie puppies are curious, alert, busy explorers. Your puppy will be eager to investigate his new home. Some of the characteristics you admire most about your new friend—his natural inquisitiveness and small size—also create some of the biggest problems for his safety.

Play it safe. "Puppy-proof" your home *before* you bring your Sheltie home. Check your house, garage, yard, and garden thoroughly for potential puppy dangers. Even though your Sheltie will live in the house with you, be sure to check *everywhere*—inside and outdoors—for any possible hazards, and remove them or block access to them. Puppies have a way of finding trouble the moment you turn your back. If a door is left ajar, your Sheltie might wander out to the garage, yard, or street where countless dangers await him.

Be careful not to step on your Shetland Sheepdog! When you are not carrying or confining him, he will probably be right underfoot. One of the most common causes of puppy injuries is being stepped on, often resulting in broken bones. Owners can trip over their puppies and be injured as well.

SHOPPING LIST

What Your Shetland Sheepdog Needs

✔ **Collar:** Use a small collar such as a break-away collar to help a very young Sheltie get used to the feel of wearing one. Later, your puppy can wear a nylon or leather collar for training. Check the collar often to make sure it is not too tight. You should be able to comfortably slip one or two fingers under the collar. Never use a slip collar on your Sheltie unless you are directly supervising him from the other end of the leash.

✔ **Identification tag:** Be sure to include your telephone number and an alternate contact telephone number in case you cannot be reached.

✔ **Leash:** A light leash is all that is necessary for a Sheltie puppy. Do not use retractable leashes. They are not good training tools. When your puppy enrolls in a training class, use a 5- or 6-foot (1.5–1.8 m) leather or nylon leash. They are helpful for teaching your Sheltie to come to you (see Chapter 7, "Training and Activities").

✔ **Dishes:** Buy food and water dishes made of stainless steel or ceramic. They can be easily cleaned and disinfected and cannot be chewed. Do not use plastic or rubber dishes. They can cause skin irritation, especially on the chin and lips.

✔ **Food:** Feed top-quality puppy food. Consult your veterinarian and your puppy's breeder for recommendations.

✔ **Bed, pillows, blankets:** Purchase bedding material made of natural material, such as cotton or wool.

✔ **Crate (Travel kennel):** The crate must be large enough for your Sheltie to sit, stand, and turn around comfortably.

✔ **Exercise pen (x-pen):** Exercise pens provide a safe enclosure for puppies to play and exercise under supervision. They are portable, folding pens, available in a variety of sizes. Make sure the wire spacing is close enough so that your Sheltie does not injure a foot or limb by catching it between the wires. Recommended size for Shelties: 2 feet high (61 cm).

✔ **Safety gates:** Safety gates are useful barriers to prevent escape or injury. Use noncollapsing, nonfolding safety gates to prevent pinching and crushing accidents.

✔ **Grooming table:** Grooming table with nonslip surface.

✔ **Grooming supplies:** Slicker brush or stiff bristle brush, wide-toothed metal comb, fine-toothed metal comb, blunt-tipped scissors, nail trimmers, styptic powder, puppy shampoo, conditioning rinse, gentle ear-cleaning solution, cotton balls, talcum powder, soft toothbrush, toothpaste formulated for dogs.

✔ **Toys:** Offer soft stuffed toys, balls, and indestructible chew toys. Avoid toys with small bells, whistles, buttons, or other items that can be a choking hazard.

✔ **Housetraining pads:** Housetraining pads are available from pet stores.

✔ **Scooper:** "Pooper scoopers" are available from pet stores in various sizes.

✔ **First aid kit:** See contents for first aid kit in Chapter 6, "Health and Nutrition."

When you first bring your Sheltie home, do not give him full access to all areas of your house. Keep him safe by restricting him to an easy-to-clean, comfortable area where he can see you and be part of the family activities, and where it is easy for you to observe him.

Closely supervise your Shetland Sheepdog's activities at all times.

Puppy-Proofing Checklist

✔ **Look for potential dangers:** Your safe home can be a very dangerous place for a baby Sheltie! Drop down low to your Sheltie's point of view to see what kind of trouble your puppy could encounter.

✔ **Doors, windows, furniture:** Make sure all doors are securely closed so your Sheltie does not wander into the garage, where he might find poisonous chemicals; or be lost outdoors, where he can be injured or killed by aggressive animals or moving vehicles. Prevent your Sheltie from jumping or climbing up on furniture, so he is not injured from falling off of furniture or falling out of an open window. Make sure that pull cords for draperies and blinds are not within your pet's reach. Puppies love to play with cords, but can quickly become entangled in, and strangled by, dangling cords and loops. Keep your Sheltie away from rocking, gliding, and reclining chairs to avoiding crushing injuries.

✔ **Cabinets:** Securely fasten cabinets containing household cleaning products, chemicals, and medicines. Make sure nothing can fall off shelves onto your puppy.

✔ **Baseboards and walls:** Prevent your puppy from chewing on baseboards and walls. Some older buildings may have been painted with toxic paints or varnishes.

✔ **Electrical cords, equipment, and appliances:** Unplug and remove electrical cords so that your puppy cannot chew on them. Electrocution, burns, and death from gnawing on electrical cords are, unfortunately, common pet accidents. Exposed wires can also start an electrical fire in your home.

✔ **Kitchen:** Put up a barrier (such as a safe, noncollapsible, noncrushing baby gate) to prevent your puppy from entering the kitchen while you are cooking. Pet injuries, such as burns from accidental cooking spills, and crushing injuries from being stepped on, occur often in the kitchen.

✔ **Bathroom:** Remove chemical toilet cleaners and keep the lids down on toilets so your pet cannot drink out of them. Make sure all medicines and toiletries are stored in securely fastened cabinets.

✔ **Garage:** Check for sharp objects, tools, poisons, chemicals, insecticides, rodent baits, and snap traps (these can break your Sheltie's toes and injure his nose). Antifreeze (ethylene glycol), often dripped onto garage floors, has a sweet taste and is a common cause of animal poisoning. Even a very small amount can cause severe kidney damage and death.

✔ **Yard hazards:** Check for holes in and under the fence; gates that do not close or latch securely; sharp objects, garden tools, and sprinkler heads; and toxic chemicals, including pesticides, rodent baits, fertilizers, weed killers, and poison mulch (such as cocoa mulch).

✔ **Poisonous plants:** Most ornamental house and garden plants are poisonous. If you are not certain about the toxicity of specific plants, check with your local nursery.

✔ **Foreign objects:** Small balls, children's toys, whistles, rubber bands, paper clips, pens, sewing needles, string, pieces of plastic, bottle caps, coins, and countless other items can be toxic or obstruct the airways, throat, or intestinal tract. Pennies contain high levels of zinc and can cause zinc poisoning as well as choking.

✔ **Garbage:** Puppies love to explore trash and will chew on and eat spoiled food, bones, plastic, aluminum, and other dangerous items. "Garbage poisoning" is a common form of food poisoning in dogs. It is caused by bacteria and bacterial toxins found in old and decaying foods.

✔ **Candies, gums, foods, medicines:** Hard or chewy candies can lodge between the teeth at the back of the jaw or in the throat and cause choking and suffocation. Chocolate contains theobromine, a methylxanthine substance, similar to caffeine, that is toxic for dogs. (Cocoa mulch also contains this toxic chemical.) Many sugar-free gums and sugar-free diet foods contain xylitol, an artificial sweetener that causes acute toxicity in dogs by inducing a sudden drop in blood sugar that leads to rapid death. Grapes and raisins can cause severe kidney damage and death in dogs. An overdose of common medicines, including thyroxin, aspirin, acetaminophen (Tylenol), ibuprofen (Advil, Motrin), and naproxen (Aleve), can also be fatal for your Sheltie.

✔ **Swimming pools and whirlpool tubs:** To prevent possible drowning, keep pools and whirlpool tubs covered, build an emergency escape ramp, make sure there are no openings in the fence around pools and spas, keep the gate closed, and do not allow your Sheltie to have access to these areas. As soon as your puppy is *old enough to learn and swim well*, train him where the pool's stairs and exit are and how to find and reach them, in case he ever falls in by accident.

CAUTION

Foods Toxic for Your Sheltie

Grapes and raisins: Just a few grapes or raisins can cause severe kidney damage and death.

Chocolate: Chocolate contains a methylxanthine substance, similar to caffeine, called theobromine that is toxic to dogs.

Xylitol, an artificial sweetener: Xylitol is found in sugar-free candies, gum, and some baked goods. It causes a sudden drop in a dog's blood sugar and rapid death.

Welcome Home!

Ideally, the breeder will have already introduced your Shetland Sheepdog puppy to a crate as part of his basic preliminary training *before* you bring him home. A crate makes an ideal "den" for Sheltie puppies. If your puppy is unfamiliar with a crate, then now is the perfect time to introduce him to one. You will use a crate often, for travel, home, and training.

Place your Sheltie's favorite toy or a blanket with familiar scents (such as a blanket that his mother and littermates slept on) in the crate for the trip home. A familiar item with comforting smells will help your puppy feel more secure while he travels and during his first days in his new home with you.

The trip from the breeder's to your home may be the first time your puppy has ever traveled in a car. Give him a chance to urinate and defecate before you place him in the crate. If food is withheld for an hour before the trip, your puppy will be less likely to become carsick. Many puppies are carsick for their first few car rides. If your Sheltie feels nauseated, he may drool or vomit, so bring plenty of paper towels and a trash bag for the trip home, just in case.

Important: Do not withhold food or water from your puppy for long periods of time or he could become hypoglycemic (have low blood sugar) and dehydrated and become weak and sick.

When you arrive home, give your puppy a small drink of water. Place him in an area that you want him to use for urination and defecation, and give him some time to relax, explore, and do his "potty" business. Then

praise him profusely for eliminating in the right spot. Congratulations! You have just successfully completed your Sheltie's first travel lesson and house-training lesson. That was easy!

Your Sheltie is just a baby, and he will be very tired from the trip and excitement. If he is sleepy, let him rest. If he is interested in becoming better acquainted, do so calmly and gently. Avoid loud noises and sudden movements. If you have children in the home, teach them to respect the puppy's space and privacy, to speak in soft voices, and to not make sudden movements that might frighten him.

Set up a safe area near the kitchen or living room where your puppy can be safe, warm, and protected and you can easily observe him. You can use baby gates, barriers, or exercise pens to make a secure enclosure. Place a water bowl in the enclosed area, and keep fresh, clean water available for him at all times.

Remove the door from the crate when you use the crate as a den for your Sheltie. Do not leave the door of the crate open, because your puppy's feet can get caught and pinched between the crate and the hinged side of the open door. Place the crate inside the enclosed area and place soft bedding inside of the crate. Add interesting toys and little bits of food treats. The crate should always be a pleasant place to be. Let your puppy explore and relax for several minutes. When he enters the crate on his own, praise him. Eventually he will go in and out of the crate as he pleases and will use the crate as a safe den for privacy and to sleep. Congratulations! You have just successfully completed the first stage of crate training. That was easy, too!

Continue to feed your Sheltie puppy the same food that the breeder was feeding him. Do not change his diet suddenly, as this could upset his digestive system. If you want to change the type of food your puppy is eating, do it gradually. Ask your veterinarian about the best food for your puppy and the correct amount to feed.

Feed your puppy *small, frequent meals* throughout the day. Depending on age, growth, and activity level, your puppy may need four to six small meals daily. You can also feed him free choice (*ad libitum*) if he is not greedy and doesn't tend to overeat. Your puppy's food should always be fresh daily.

Shelties grow rapidly during the first six months of life. When your puppy is about 12 to 20 weeks of age, you can feed him four meals daily. At about six months of age, he can be switched to an adult feeding schedule of two meals daily, 12 hours apart.

As your puppy grows and matures, his nutritional needs will change and you will vary his diet accordingly. Be sure to consult your veterinarian to be certain his feeding schedule and diet matches his specific needs. Measure your puppy's food and water so you know exactly how much he eats and drinks every day. Weigh your puppy once a week.

Crate Training

CAUTION

Slip or choke collars are not safe for Shelties *until they are older and have been trained to this type of collar.* Never leave your puppy unattended wearing a slip or choke collar. The collar could accidentally catch on something and your puppy could strangle.

Crate training is a very important part of your Shetland Sheepdog's basic, early education. Make it fun! Teach your Sheltie that his crate is a place of his own: safe, private, and comfortable.

Your Sheltie must be crate trained so that you can take him out for socialization; take him with you on vacation; go to play at dog parks, beaches, and gatherings; attend dog shows and events; go to the veterinarian; and escape with you in case you have to evacuate from your home in an emergency or disaster. Whether you travel by car, plane, train, or boat, your Sheltie must be crate trained so he can travel with you.

You already started crate training when you brought your puppy home and introduced the crate to him for use as a secure den without a door. Now it is time for him to learn to be crated with the door closed. Start by placing the crate in a safe area where your Sheltie feels secure and can watch the family activities—and where you can keep an eye on him as well.

Don't put your puppy's crate in an area where he will feel isolated. Sheltie puppies want to see everything that is going on around them. Exposure to various sights, sounds, smells, activities, and people are very important aspects of your puppy's socialization.

To start crate training, play with your puppy so that he has a chance to exercise, eliminate, and perhaps feel a little sleepy after all the activity. Calmly put him in the crate with a special toy and a treat, and close the crate door. Make the house quiet and leave your puppy in the crate for 10 minutes. Let him watch you as you go about your normal activities during these ten minutes. If your Sheltie barks or cries while he is in his crate, ignore the noise. If you respond by letting him out, he will think he is being rewarded for barking. Your Sheltie may simply take a nap, but if he stays awake and remains quiet, let him out of the crate after 10 minutes and praise him. Repeat this procedure once every day or two. Using this method, you can gradually extend the time an additional five minutes every few days, up to one hour. Never confine your Shetland Sheepdog in a crate for extended periods of time. If you do, it will seem more like a prison to him than a pleasant place to be.

Housetraining

Shetland Sheepdogs are naturally very clean dogs. They are also highly intelligent. Compared with most other breeds, Shelties are easy to housetrain. Shelties try hard not to soil their homes, dens, or sleeping areas. If your puppy has an "accident," it is because he was forced to wait longer than he was capable of waiting. The solution is simple. Take your puppy outside to relieve himself more often.

Breed Truths

Shelties are naturally very clean dogs, and they are easily housetrained. Shelties try hard not to have an accident in their living area, so if you are vigilant and help your puppy go to the right spot at the right moment, he will be housetrained within a reasonable time period.

Keys to successful housetraining:

1. Watch closely for signs that your puppy needs to go outside.
2. Keep a regular schedule to go outside.
3. Keep a regular feeding schedule.
4. Always take your puppy to the same area to eliminate.

Young puppies have very small bladders and lack full bladder control. Ideally your Sheltie should go outside every two hours when you first start housetraining him. Of course, there will be times when you simply cannot do this. When you have to be out of the house for a few hours, you can restrict your puppy to a designated, safe, easy-to-clean, confined area. Cover the floor with newspapers or housetraining pads. Puppies tend to wander about as they urinate or defecate, so cover as much of the floor as possible. If you live in an area where weather prohibits taking your puppy outside (snow, rain, cold wind, extreme heat, hot asphalt and sidewalks), his paper training will come in handy.

BE PREPARED! Housetraining Essentials

1. Start housetraining your Shetland Sheepdog the day he arrives—it is never too early.
2. Make sure your puppy is receiving good nutrition, has normal stools, and is free of internal parasites.
3. Keep your Shetland Sheepdog on a regular feeding schedule.
4. Let your puppy outside several times a day: first thing in the morning, after every meal, after naps, throughout the day, and right before bedtime.
5. *Never scold or hit your puppy if he has an accident in the house. Never!*
6. Watch for behavioral signs that your puppy needs to go outside.
7. Be patient, kind, and consistent in your training.
8. Praise your Shetland Sheepdog enthusiastically when he does the right thing.

Start your puppy's training right by taking him to his designated toilet area when you first bring him home. Place him in the area you want him to learn to use. Introduce a training key word, such as *potty*, and use it whenever you take your puppy outside to relieve himself. When your Sheltie is finished, praise him enthusiastically and give him a small food reward so he knows you are pleased.

Helpful Hints

Signs that a puppy has to urinate or defecate include sniffing the ground, pacing, circling, running back and forth, whining, crying, and acting anxious. Take your Sheltie outside to eliminate the moment you see this behavior!

As soon as your puppy *understands* that he should urinate or defecate only in the area you have indicated, he will try his best to use that spot. If that area is outside, he will have to wait until you take him there. Don't wait for your puppy to tell you he needs to go. He will not yet know *how* to tell you. It is up to you to be attentive to his needs and signs of impending urination or defecation so you can take him to his toilet area in time.

If your Sheltie eliminates in the "wrong" place, remember it is just an accident and not intentional. Do not punish him. Simply clean up the mess. *Never raise your voice or shout or use physical punishment of any kind.* That is the worst thing you can do. Your Sheltie is only a baby with little control at this time. Everything is new and strange, and he will not associate your scolding with his natural body functions. He will be especially confused if you reprimand him several minutes after he had the accident. Shelties are very sensitive dogs that try hard to please their people. If you speak harshly to your puppy, he will be startled and confused. He may become less sociable or withdraw from you.

Helpful Hints

Work on positive reinforcement. Praise your puppy profusely when he does the right thing so he knows he has pleased you. You will be surprised at how quickly he learns!

Never use the crate as a tool for punishment or isolation. Do not put your Sheltie in the crate when he has misbehaved. If you do, he will associate his crate with punishment and unhappiness and will not want to use it.

When your Sheltie is used to being in his crate for up to two hours, you can take advantage of his crate training to complement his housetraining. At night, place lots of absorbent bedding in the crate and place the crate in your bedroom so you can hear your puppy when he wakes up and needs to go. In the beginning, this may be as often as every two hours.

When you take your puppy out during the night, do not play with him. Be patient. Say "Potty" and give him 10 to 15 minutes (he probably won't take that long) and *wait* with him. Do not go back into the house and leave him outside alone. Your puppy will worry and spend his time looking for you, rather than doing what he was let outside to do. If you are not outside with your puppy, you won't know if he did anything. It's important to know if your puppy is having trouble, is in pain, is constipated, has diarrhea, or has blood or parasites in his feces. You will not know unless you are watching him.

Note: If your puppy has a problem, collect a fresh stool specimen to take to your veterinarian for diagnosis.

After your puppy is finished, be sure to praise him. Take him back inside and return him to his crate. *Make sure his crate is large enough for him to stand, sit, and turn around comfortably. Do not keep him in a crate for more than two to three hours at a time and do not exceed a total crate time of six hours each evening.*

CAUTION

If your Shetland Sheepdog (puppy or adult) is well housetrained and starts having accidents in the house, this could be a sign of health problems such as a bladder infection, intestinal upset, incontinence, or stress. Consult your veterinarian.

It's not easy, but successful housetraining means that you will have to get up as needed during the night and in the early morning hours to let your puppy out to eliminate. It is cruel and unfair for you to sleep in while your puppy waits miserably with full bladder and bowels for you to take him outside. Also, if puppies have to hold their urine for excessive periods of time, they can be more prone to developing bladder infections.

If crating your puppy at night is not practical for you, you can instead confine him to a designated area and cover the floor with newspapers so he can relieve himself during the night without soiling his sleeping area. Eventually your puppy will be able to wait for longer periods of time as he develops more bowel and bladder control. Be patient! It will be a while before he can hold his bladder and bowels overnight.

Litter Boxes

Some Shetland Sheepdog puppies can be trained to use a large litter box indoors and may continue to use them when they are adults. This may be a suitable option for when you are unable to return home in time to let your Sheltie out or when you are traveling with him. It is also practical for sick or elderly animals that have urinary or bowel incontinence problems.

You can make or buy a shallow litter box (2 to 4 inches [5–10 cm] deep) that is about 12 by 12 inches (30.5 by 30.5 cm) square or larger. A wide variety of litter material is available from pet stores, including clean sand, paper pellets, shredded paper litter, and wood pellets or shavings. *Do not use clumping cat litter*. Take a tiny amount of feces from your puppy's last bowel movement and place it in the litter box. Put the litter box in your pet's enclosure. When your puppy acts like he needs to relieve himself, quickly place him in the box. When he eliminates in the box, praise him enthusiastically and give him a small food reward.

Helpful Hints

You can teach your Shetland Sheepdog to ring a bell to ask to go outside. Fasten a squeaker toy or bell to your door, within your pet's reach. Every time you take him outside, squeak the toy, or ring the bell, immediately before leaving the house. He will quickly associate the sound with going outside and doing his toilet business. But be forewarned: Your Sheltie is smart! He might also use this new trick to ask to go outside just to play!

Housetraining requires two-way communication. You teach your Shetland Sheepdog that he must eliminate outside and he must find a way to let you know his desire to go outside. Your puppy may never "ask" to go outside, by barking or scratching at the door or fetching his leash like the dogs in the movies. But if he hasn't been outside for a long period of time, or just woke up, or just finished eating, or acts anxious and starts to pant and stare at you, then you know what to do.

House Rules

Your Shetland Sheepdog puppy must learn the house rules. Decide what you are willing, or unwilling, to allow your puppy to do. For example, if you do not want your pet in a certain area of the home or garden, or on the furniture, or sleeping on your bed, you have to teach him the limits when he is young. If you let him do these things when he is a puppy, he will naturally think it is all right to do them when he is an adult.

There are a lot of rules for a puppy to learn, so be patient and give him time. Here are a dozen basic house rules for puppies:

1. **Boundaries:** Teach your Sheltie where he is allowed in the house and yard and which areas are off limits. Do not give your puppy too much freedom too soon. Use exercise pens and gates to limit areas, and gradually expand them as he is housetrained, socialized, and formally trained.
2. *Come:* Teach your puppy to come when he is called. For his safety, this should be one of the first things your Sheltie learns to do.
3. **Barking:** Shelties like to bark! Teach your puppy that excessive barking is not permissible.
4. **Chewing:** Teach your Sheltie to chew only on chew toys you give him.
5. **Begging:** No begging! Keep your Sheltie out of the kitchen and dining area during mealtimes.
6. **Crate:** Your Sheltie should be calm and quiet in his crate.
7. **Housetraining:** Teach your Sheltie to go outside or to a designated area to urinate and defecate.
8. **Manners:** Jumping up on people and furniture is not allowed.
9. **Household items:** Do not let your Sheltie chew on carpets or furniture, dig in potted plants, or rummage through the trash.
10. *Wait:* Your Shetland Sheepdog must learn to wait for permission from you before he does something. For example, he should sit and wait to go outside until you give him permission. Don't allow him to dart out the door or to pull you on a leash. Teach him to wait for meals, by sitting politely until you lower the food bowl and give him the signal that he can eat.
11. *Drop it* or *Leave it:* Teach your Shetland Sheepdog to release an item in his mouth that you do not want him to have.
12. **Biting or nipping:** Your puppy must learn that biting is forbidden.

Socializing Your Sheltie Puppy

Your new puppy needs lots of socialization—every day—so that he can grow to his full potential as a confident, friendly, and well-adjusted Shetland Sheepdog.

The most critical time period for socialization in a puppy's life is from 3 weeks to 12 weeks of age, with 3 weeks to 8 weeks of age being the most influential period. This means that it is your puppy's breeder's responsibility to give your puppy and his littermates lots of socialization during this critical time period, before placing the puppies in homes. From 7 to 9 weeks of age, puppies become especially responsive to humans and thrive on attention. By 9 weeks of age, most puppies' personalities are well set and have been greatly influenced by the amount of human contact, handling, petting, and positive interactions they experienced. If a puppy is ignored

BE PREPARED! Puppy Classes

Many dog clubs, trainers, and pet stores offer puppy classes. These "classes" are not formal instruction classes, although puppies learn some basic commands such as *sit* and *come*. Puppy classes introduce puppies to strangers, new situations, and structured playtime with other puppies in a new environment. Puppy classes build a puppy's confidence and social skills during a critically formative time in the puppy's life.

PERSONALITY POINTERS
Common Puppy Behavior Problems

Problem	What to Do
Barking	Shelties love to bark! Do not reward your puppy when he barks for no apparent reason. Distract him and ask him to do something, such as *sit*. When he has stopped barking and done what you asked him to do, praise him and give him a treat.
Biting	Do not allow your puppy to play bite or chew on your fingers. Say, "Ouch! No!" Stop playing and distract him. Offer him a chew toy.
Chewing	Do not allow your puppy to chew on anything except chew toys. Tell him *Drop it* or *Leave it* and remove the object.
Jumping	Do not pick your puppy up and cuddle him when he jumps on people or furniture. Distract him from the undesirable behavior by telling him to *sit*. Make sure he sits in place for at least a few seconds, and then praise him.

or neglected, he will have social difficulties all of his life, many that cannot be resolved or overcome.

Shelties should not be placed in new homes before the age of 8 weeks. Some breeders wait until their puppies are 11 to 12 weeks of age before they sell them. This means that your Sheltie will probably be 8 weeks of age or older when you acquire him. It will be very important to continue your puppy's socialization training throughout his life and especially between 8 and 11 weeks of age during the "fear imprint period" (see Chapter 5, "Living with a Shetland Sheepdog" for socialization methods).

Introduce your puppy to new people, places, situations, and things—but not all at once! Make sure his experiences are positive ones. Early and continual socialization will make your Shetland Sheepdog confident and also help him cope with unexpected, noisy, and frightening events such as thunderstorms, fire alarms, and fireworks.

Puppy Health and Nutrition

Your Shetland Sheepdog's health care starts from birth. Your puppy depends on you to feed him the best food and give him the best care possible to keep him healthy from the first day you bring him home—and for the rest of his life. Good health care and nutrition mean fewer health problems and a longer life span for your companion.

Give your puppy lots of love and attention. A stressed puppy is prone to illnesses, so socialize your puppy well and spend lots of time with him.

Exercise is important. Play games with your puppy and take him on little walks. Keep in mind that while he is very small, your puppy has to take several steps for every one of your steps.

Shetland Sheepdog puppies need regular grooming, just like adults do. Brushing keeps the skin healthy and the coat beautiful. Brush your puppy's coat daily so it can grow into the gorgeous full coat for which Shetland Sheepdogs are known. When you brush your puppy's coat, check for mats, parasites, and skin sores.

Take your puppy to your veterinarian for a health checkup within 72 hours of bringing him home. Use his crate to transport him to the doctor's office, and bring a large towel or small baby blanket with you. After the exam table has been disinfected, place the towel/blanket on the tabletop and set him on it while your veterinarian conducts the physical examination. That way your puppy will not get cold from the table top and

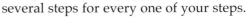

Helpful Hints

Puppies usually urinate immediately after waking up from a nap and defecate right after eating. In these situations, take your Shetland Sheepdog directly to his toilet area without waiting for signs. Remember to always praise him enthusiastically for his good performance.

will not come in contact with germs from other animals that were previously on the table. Your puppy is not fully protected against some contagious diseases until he has had his third set of vaccinations (around 16 weeks of age).

Your veterinarian will conduct a physical examination on your new puppy. This includes checking for internal and external parasites; listening to your puppy's heart and lungs; palpating the lymph nodes and body organs; and checking your puppy's eyes, ears, nose, mouth, and throat. Your veterinarian will weigh your Sheltie and make feeding recommendations, discuss health care and parasite control, review a vaccination schedule, and answer your questions. You may decide to have your Sheltie vaccinated or microchipped at that time.

Your Sheltie puppy's stomach is too small to hold enough food in a single meal to supply his daily caloric needs and support his growth, development,

FYI: Basic Puppy Care at Home

- Brush your Sheltie's coat daily.
- Check inside your puppy's ears. If they are dirty, clean them gently with a soft, damp cloth. Do not use ear cleaners containing alcohol. They can burn and irritate tender ears.
- Practice brushing your Sheltie's teeth with a soft toothbrush once a week. Although your puppy will lose his baby (deciduous) teeth by the time he is six or seven months of age, brushing the baby teeth now teaches your Sheltie to let you brush his teeth so you can continue his dental care when he is an adult.
- Trim the very tips of your puppy's nails once a week.

and activity level. He must eat small meals—several of them—throughout the day. He needs a special diet, specifically developed for puppies, with a good balance of high-quality protein, fats, and carbohydrates. One of the best things you can do for your Sheltie is feed him a high-quality dog food.

A scale is a wise investment. If you weigh your puppy once a week and record his weight, you will be able to accurately monitor his growth rate and adjust his diet, with help from your veterinarian, to maintain your Sheltie at an ideal weight to keep him healthy.

CAUTION

Dog feces and urine may contain contagious organisms that can spread diseases (such as parvovirus, intestinal parasites, *Leptospira*). Some of these are contagious to other dogs, and some are contagious to people. The common canine roundworm can cause serious health problems in children. When you take your pet outside, take a plastic bag or a "pooper scooper" to promptly pick up the mess, and discard it properly in a well-sealed plastic bag. Don't bury the excrement in the ground where it can be stepped on or where other animals can find it.

Puppy Vaccinations

Vaccination is a medical decision, not a calendar event. The type of vaccination, and when it is given, are decisions you will make together with your veterinarian, based on your puppy's age, health, and potential risk of exposure. There are significant benefits, as well as some risks, associated with any vaccine.

Your veterinarian may recommend extending the time interval between vaccines by a few days or a few weeks, rather than giving all the vaccines at one time. By spacing some of the vaccinations, your puppy's immune system may respond better and the chances of adverse vaccine reactions may be reduced.

In 2011, the American Veterinary Medical Association and the American Animal Hospital Association published new canine preventive health-care

HOME BASICS
Sample Vaccination Schedule for Core Vaccines

The following vaccination schedule should be considered only as a guideline.

Vaccine	1st inoculation Age	2nd inoculation Age	3rd inoculation Age	1st Booster Interval	Follow up Interval
Distemper	8 weeks	12 weeks	16 weeks	1 year	To be determined by veterinarian, may be 3 years
Canine adenovirus-2 Hepatitis	8 weeks	12 weeks	16 weeks	1 year	To be determined by veterinarian, may be 3 years
Parvovirus	8 weeks	12 weeks	16 weeks	1 year	To be determined by veterinarian, may be 3 years
Rabies	12 weeks to 16 weeks (state laws vary)			1 year	State laws vary, in most states every 3 years

guidelines designed to improve pet health (see Resources). This includes the most recent Canine Vaccine Guidelines.

Your Sheltie may need other vaccinations, such as one for "kennel cough" (*Bordetella bronchiseptica*), or Lyme disease (*Borrelia burgdorferi*), depending upon risk of exposure (boarding, dog classes, dog shows, dog parks). Which vaccines to give and how often will be determined by your veterinarian according to your pet's particular circumstances.

Guideline for "kennel cough" Bordetella vaccine: Begin with an intranasal administration followed in two to four weeks with an injectable booster and then an injectable booster every six months (or annually), depending upon the risk of exposure (boarding, dog classes, dog shows, dog parks).

Helpful Hints

When you take your Sheltie puppy to your veterinarian, do not act like you are worried about him or feel sorry for him. This teaches your puppy to be afraid of his veterinarian. Instead, be reassuring and matter-of-fact, and praise your puppy for his brave behavior. This will help him build confidence.

73

Chapter Five

Living with a Shetland Sheepdog

Your Sheltie is the product of countless generations of selective breeding that have produced a highly intelligent herding dog—and the most devoted of companions. Herding instinct, intense loyalty, sound temperament, and a gentle disposition are indelibly etched into your Sheltie's genetic makeup.

Athletic, energetic, robust, and enthusiastic, Shelties are seemingly tireless when it comes to work or play. Nothing pleases a Sheltie more than having a job to do and pleasing his owner. Shelties are canine perfectionists. *If* your Sheltie understands and knows what you are asking of him, he will do it to the best of his ability. He will put his heart into everything he does, just for the pure joy of pleasing you.

Shetland Sheepdogs are independent thinkers and rank among the most intelligent and most trainable of canine breeds. They may well be the most willing, adaptable, and versatile breed in existence today. Although Shelties were bred and raised primarily as farm dogs used to herd sheep, they use their instinct, intelligence, and problem-solving skills in creative ways. There are reports in the literature of Shelties doing a fine job herding various animals, including cattle, goats, and fowl. So if your Sheltie has a keen herding instinct, don't be surprised if he has a tendency to herd children and other family pets. For a Sheltie, making sure the family is safely gathered and all is right with the world is just one of his many important, self-assigned jobs.

There are as many stories testifying to the Sheltie's abilities, intelligence, and communication skills as there are Shelties. One story (Coleman, 1943) recounts how a farmer told a visitor that he planned to put certain sheep in a given pen the following day. In the morning, the farmer discovered that his Shetland Sheepdog had already gone down to the fold and herded the individually specified sheep into the designated pen! Of course, the assumption was that the Sheltie had understood the entire conversation. You decide!

Shelties have a great ability to form associations between facial expressions, movements, phrases, activities, scents, and other cues, and learn quickly. Your Sheltie will watch your every move and listen very closely to you. It can be a bit eerie living with a dog that seems to understand everything you say, that is often able to predict your next move, and that appears at times to read your mind. Your Sheltie's mysterious abilities stem from his attentiveness, observation skills, ability to integrate and process information, memory retention, intelligence—and the amount of time you spend with him in play, training, and interactive activities. Your Sheltie is the result of generations of selective breeding, but it is up to you to help him blossom to his full potential and be the ultimate companion and working partner.

Shelties are not clingy dogs. They love attention, but they do not constantly demand attention from their owners. Shelties quickly learn to respect their owner's privacy and space. If you have things you need to do, your Sheltie can learn to wait calmly while you go about your business. When you can include your Sheltie in your activities, though, it is much more fun for both of you! Even if you are simply working at your desk, your Sheltie will be happiest if he can be nearby and watch you. Then, as soon as you are ready to take a break, go for a walk or car ride, or simply play a game, your Sheltie will be at your side and eager to join you.

Bonding

You have brought a Shetland Sheepdog into your home—and into your life. This means that your Sheltie will be part of your family and you will form a strong bond of trust and friendship with him. In return for your long-term commitment, your Sheltie will bring you many years of companionship and happiness.

Some owners tend to treat their Shelties more like little surrogate children than like dogs. Perhaps this is because Shetland Sheepdogs bond so closely with their owners, understand so much, and are so smart. But there are also biological components to this intriguing human-animal bond relationship. Research has shown that babylike facial features can stimulate activity in a specific part of the brain involved in emotional responses that can trigger the equivalent of parental instincts. Just looking at a puppy can trigger a "nurturing response" in humans. Something as simple as making eye contact with one's own dog can cause the brain to release oxytocin, a hormone that plays an important role in maternal bonding, trust, desire for social connection, and stress reduction. Researchers discovered that when people pet their dogs, oxytocin is released in humans *and* their dogs. So if you think you are happier and feel better after petting your Sheltie, you are right!

Fun Facts

Studies have shown that dog ownership can have many health benefits. Research indicates that people who own dogs live longer than people who do not. Owning a canine companion can help prevent loneliness, reduce depression, and improve immunity. Simply petting a dog can help slow heart rate and lower blood pressure.

Leader of the Pack

Shelties accept their owners as being the "pack leader." Just as your Sheltie's ancestors took their working instructions from crofters in the fields, your Sheltie looks to you for cues, guidance, training, and praise. You are in charge as the pack leader. Your Sheltie is comfortable in his role of being the subordinate and looks to you for direction.

To be consistent in training and to keep from confusing your Sheltie, everyone in the family has to be in agreement about house rules. For example, if your family has agreed to limit treats to a certain amount, then *everyone* has to follow the rules. If one member of the family falls victim to your Sheltie's sweet expression, weakens, and gives in, then your dog will know exactly who to go to every time he begs for food. That also won't help your image as pack leader! In addition to lack of consistency and interfering with training progress, your Sheltie can become overweight if he eats too many treats. There are good reasons why many Sheltie owners end up spelling words (such as t-r-e-a-t) when speaking to family members while their Sheltie is present in the room.

For your Sheltie to become the exemplary canine citizen you want him to be, he must be properly socialized, learn to understand and obey commands, and respect limits and boundaries. This will enable him to grow into the overall mentally balanced and well-mannered dog for which Shetland Sheepdogs are recognized.

Living with such an extraordinarily bright and devoted dog will surely be one of your most treasured lifetime experiences. Shelties bond closely

FYI: Responsibilities of Owning a Sheltie

Owning and living with a Shetland Sheepdog is a wonderful experience, but it comes with many responsibilities, including common neighborhood courtesy. Make sure your Sheltie doesn't become a neighborhood nuisance by escaping into your neighbors' yards, or a liability by running loose in the streets where he could cause an accident. Take care to ensure that he doesn't disturb your neighbors with excessive barking. When you take your Sheltie out for walks, keep him on a leash, and be sure to clean up his excrement and discard it. Check with your local animal regulatory authorities about dog-licensing requirements, and keep your Sheltie's license and tags current.

with their owners and are very sensitive to human emotions and moods. The companionship and happiness that your Sheltie will bring you will be immeasurable. He will prove to be one of the sweetest, most affectionate, cleverest, and most obedient dogs you will ever love—and one of the best friends you will ever have.

A Long-Term Commitment

When you brought your Sheltie into your life, you essentially made several promises to him. You made a pledge to give him lots of love, time, and attention; a safe, comfortable home; socialization; room to play and plenty of exercise; training; regular grooming; veterinary care as needed; and the best food and care possible for his entire life. Shetland Sheepdogs can live up to 15 years or more, so you made a very big long-term commitment!

Breed Needs

Your Sheltie needs

1. lots of love, time, and attention from you and interactive play;
2. a high-quality puppy or dog food according to his age and activity;
3. socialization;
4. exercise;
5. training;
6. identification with a microchip *and* a collar with tag;
7. regular veterinary checkups, vaccinations, and parasite control;
8. frequent, regular grooming;
9. lots of activities and toys; and
10. safe, comfortable housing.

Shelties and Children

Children are naturally drawn to Shelties. They simply cannot resist a Sheltie's sweet expression, endearing appearance, small size, and calm demeanor. Children love to pet animals, and the Sheltie's beautiful coat is a delight to touch. Shelties are very good with children, and a well-socialized Sheltie makes an excellent companion for a child, especially older children.

Teach children in the family the correct way to hold and handle your Sheltie puppy. Demonstrate the correct way to gently lift your puppy, by placing one hand under his hindquarters and the other hand under his chest and abdomen for support. Many children are too small, or have hands too small, to hold a puppy without dropping him. It is safer for these children to sit on the floor, under adult supervision, and hold the puppy on their lap.

Shelties are naturally kind and gentle with children. They are not aggres-

CAUTION

Children must learn to
- not lift a Sheltie by his legs. He could be dropped, or his limbs could be injured, dislocated, or broken.
- not lift a Sheltie by the nape of the neck (skin on the back of the neck). If the puppy struggles, he could slip free and be dropped and injured.

79

BE PREPARED! Guidelines for Children

- An adult should always be present to supervise children when they interact with puppies and dogs.
- Do not give the Sheltie food or treats without permission from an adult.
- Do not startle the Sheltie if he is sleeping.
- Approach the Sheltie calmly, say his name so he knows you are there, and speak in a friendly voice. Do not shout or yell.
- Move calmly and do not suddenly lunge, grab, or clutch at the Sheltie.
- Do not squeeze or hug the dog too tightly, especially if he is a puppy.
- While holding a puppy, sit on the floor so the puppy is not accidentally dropped or injured.
- Play and have fun, but do not encourage play biting, nipping, tugging on clothing, or excessive barking.
- Be careful where you walk so you do not trip over the dog or accidentally step on him.
- Make sure to close doors carefully so you do not injure the dog and so that he does not escape. Do not take the dog outside without permission from an adult.
- *Never hit, strike, or kick a dog. Never tug or pull on a dog's ears, tail, limbs, or fur.*
- *Never tease a Sheltie.*

sive and are not likely to bite—but they can. Any dog of any breed may bite if he is accidentally mishandled, injured, in pain, startled, or frightened. Because small children are short and their heads are large in proportion to their bodies, the majority of all animal bite wounds inflicted on children happen in the area of the face and head.

Always supervise children when they play with dogs to prevent accidental injury to the child and the dog.

Your Sheltie can teach the children in your life a lot about the joys of canine friendship and loyalty, but *you* will teach the children about responsible pet ownership. By watching you, they will learn about respect for life, kindness, the importance of humane care, good nutrition, a safe home, and a kind heart.

Children may learn responsibility with time, but they cannot be held responsible for any animal's care. It is up to adults to ensure that animals receive proper care. When the novelty of a new pet wears off, children often forget their designated duties. A child may forget to clean up after an animal, or worse, forget to give food or water. Children cannot be depended upon to give a pet regular grooming or health care. As children grow, their interests change rapidly. Your Sheltie may be an important part of a child's life, or he may fall low on the child's priority list after friends, school, sports, social events, and other distractions. Then, before you know it, the children are grown and have moved out of the house, leaving the dog behind. Shelties have long life spans, so always keep in mind that although the children may be helpful now and then, your Sheltie is entirely your responsibility—for his entire life!

If a child in your family shares the same long-term enthusiasm for your Sheltie as you do, your Sheltie will give that child endless opportunities to learn about animal behavior, training, exhibiting, grooming, and care. Because Shelties are so highly trainable and so eager to please, they are ideal dogs for older children to learn how to participate, often very successfully, in canine events. They can compete in obedience, agility, and many other dog sports. A Sheltie can be a precious friend and a great confidence builder for a child. Who knows? Maybe your Sheltie will inspire some of the children he meets today to become tomorrow's Sheltie breeders, trainers, judges, and handlers!

Shelties and Other Pets

Your Sheltie will be interested in meeting all members of your family, including other household pets. He may be very friendly, right from the start, or he may act reserved or indifferent. The other animals in your home may be curious about him and friendly, or jealous, or they may not readily accept him—unless they are Shelties, too. Shelties get along well with other dogs, especially other Shelties.

A good way to start introductions is to place your Sheltie in an area of the home where he is safe from other animals, but where they can see and smell each other. For example, if you have an area near the kitchen or living room, you can place a baby bar-

CAUTION

Keep your Sheltie away from the following pets until you are certain they are compatible:

- Small mammals, such as rodents (mice, rats, hamsters, degus, guinea pigs, chinchillas), sugar gliders, rabbits, and ferrets
- Birds: A large bird could bite, peck, and claw your Sheltie and seriously injure him.
- Reptiles

Your Sheltie would not deliberately try to injure, eat, or kill these pets. However, he might think they are fabulous toys or that they would be fun to herd, or he may play too roughly with them. Most small mammal pets (ferrets and cats excluded) are prey species. The presence of a predator species (dogs) is frightening to prey species. Their instinct is to run or hide from predators, but as captives in their cages they cannot do this and may be highly stressed. Make sure the lids and doors to all of your pets' cages are securely fastened and that the cages are in a safe place.

Ferrets and cats usually adapt well to a new canine friend when given proper introductions and enough time.

rier gate to prevent your Sheltie from running loose in the house until he adapts to his new environment and your other pets are used to him.

Make sure the barrier has a mesh small enough to prevent escape or accidental injury and that your Sheltie cannot trap his head or limbs in it. You may also put him in a crate for a short time for the first few evenings so that your other household pets can approach and investigate, but cannot harm him.

Helpful Hints

Be patient, calm, and consistent in making introductions and supervising your pets. It may take several weeks before your pets are compatible.

The younger your Sheltie is, the more likely he will be to make friends with your other family pets. When you first introduce your pets, do not introduce them all at once, or one right after the other. Select one animal and make introductions calmly, slowly, and safely in a situation in which you have full control. At first, introductions should be brief. Praise and pet your animals for their good behavior.

Do everything you can to reassure your established pets that they have not lost their place in your heart. If you pet your Sheltie and make a fuss over him in their presence, they may resent him, but if you pet and praise

CAUTION

Cat claws can puncture your puppy's eyes and cause serious injury, even blindness. Always supervise your pets. For added safety, keep your cat's toenails trimmed. You can purchase easy-to-apply, soft cat-claw covers (such as Soft Paws) for added protection.

your established pets, your new Sheltie won't mind. He may, however, naturally seek your approval and praise as well.

If you own a cat, don't expect it to make friends with your Sheltie immediately. A resentful or nervous cat can inflict serious injury on an unsuspecting dog, especially a puppy. To prevent a cat-scratch eye injury (common injuries suffered by dogs) or a bite wound, do not allow your Sheltie near your cat while you are away, and supervise them closely for compatibility when you are home.

Shelties and Other Dogs

If you have one or more dogs in the home, your Sheltie puppy will probably enthusiastically welcome their company. However, adult and older dogs can be sensitive and jealous of the attention you give your Sheltie. If your dogs are happy to have a newcomer in the family and want to play, supervise them closely to be sure that they do not play too roughly.

Check for potential problems so you can prevent them before they occur. For example, if you have a dog that has a favorite toy, remove the toy before your Sheltie joins in the play. That way your Sheltie won't grab the toy and inadvertently start a quarrel. Feed your pets separately, so they do not fight over food (and so you know how much each one is eating).

Always pay extra attention to your other pets so they are not jealous of your new Sheltie. It will be a challenge dividing your time and attention among your animals and giving them all enough interactive play and affection so that each one feels it has received its fair share.

Training Basics

Training starts the first day you bring your Shetland Sheepdog home and continues throughout his entire life. The first line of communication is teaching your Sheltie his name. When he knows his name, he will know when you are talking to him. You can say his name to get his attention, then start by teaching him the basics: *come, sit, wait* (see Chapter 7, "Training and Activities"). He will also learn the meaning of "*No!*" Shelties are fast learners and fun to train. As your puppy matures, he will learn more advanced commands. These commands are important because they could possibly save your pet's life in times of emergency (*down, stay, heel* off lead).

FYI: Shetland Sheepdog Health

Shetland Sheepdogs are sturdy, robust, athletic dogs. With good care and nutrition, they can live well into their teens. Shelties need regular veterinary checkups, health care, and frequent grooming to keep skin healthy and maintain a beautiful coat. As with all breeds, there are some medical conditions to which Shelties are predisposed (see Chapter 10, "Special Considerations").

The best way to keep your Sheltie healthy is to prevent problems before they start. Give your Sheltie the best care and nutrition possible, and take him for regular veterinary checkups, routine vaccinations, and laboratory tests (to identify health problems and parasites). Shelties also need regular dental cleaning and polishing.

A very important part of canine health that has been overlooked until recent years is canine "mental well-being." A healthy Sheltie is also a mentally sound, alert, well-adjusted, and *happy* individual.

Many dogs respond to stress by developing behavior problems, such as separation anxiety, phobias, destructive chewing, and constant barking. Just like people, stressed animals are more prone to illness.

When you commit to the responsibilities of Sheltie ownership and health care, keep in mind that your Sheltie's mental well-being is a very important component of his overall health.

Breed Truths

Shelties have a good sense of property boundaries and territory. They make excellent guard dogs because they are quick to bark a warning alert if they sense danger or if a stranger approaches the home.

There are so many things a puppy must learn and remember! Here are some general rules: Do not jump on people, do not bark constantly or without reason, don't chew on the furniture, go outside to eliminate, learn to use a crate, behave in the car, stand on the grooming table, walk on a leash without pulling....The list is endless. We may not realize it, but even the basic good behavior we expect of a Sheltie, and that we so often take for granted, is, in reality, a tremendous amount for a puppy to learn and remember.

As smart as your Sheltie is, he will naturally forget and sometimes make mistakes, especially when he is young, excited, tired, or distracted. When he errs, he just needs a gentle reminder or refresher lesson to set him back on course, followed by lots of praise for his good performance. If you are consistent and clear in your training methods, you will be delighted at how much your Sheltie learns and how quickly he progresses.

Training is much more than commands and actions. Training encompasses all that it takes to create a well-mannered Sheltie that is a joy to own, travel with, and show off in public. A well trained Sheltie is the quintessential canine ambassador. He is the dog that everyone loves to know and that everyone wishes was their own. The level of training that your Sheltie attains will depend

Breed Truths

Shelties love to please their owners! They respond best and learn fastest with kind training and enthusiastic praise. Never use a harsh voice or harsh training methods when you train your Sheltie.

CHECKLIST

Keys to Socialization Training

Here are some things to introduce your Shetland Sheepdog to as part of his socialization training.

✔ Different people in a variety of clothing, hats, coats (Ask them to pet and praise your puppy.)
✔ Children of various sizes and ages
✔ Dogs, puppies, other animal species (Keep your puppy at a safe distance so he is not injured, especially by larger animals.)
✔ Different surfaces to walk on: wood, tile, carpet, grass, dirt, concrete, sand, asphalt
✔ Water: hose, sprinklers, fountains, pool, lake, beach, bathtub, rain

✔ Household appliances: hair dryer, vacuum cleaner, garbage disposal, washing machine, dryer, dishwasher, blender
✔ Unexpected movement: flags, plastic bags, kites, balloons, umbrellas
✔ Crowds: parades, events, parties, open markets, dog shows, airports
✔ Sounds: alarms, music, traffic, airports, sirens, lawn mowers, yard blowers, thunder
✔ Equipment: wheelchairs, walkers, strollers, sporting equipment, golf carts

on how well he is socialized, how much time you spend with him, your skills as a trainer, and your Sheltie's trainability.

You may discover that you and your Sheltie are great candidates for activities such as obedience, agility, rally, and other canine competitions. It takes a special partnership to accomplish high goals in competitions, and Shetland Sheepdogs were specifically selected and bred to be extraordinary working partners. It is no wonder that so many Shelties rank so high in competitive events.

Socialization

Puppies are often placed in new homes at 8 to 11 weeks of age. This age is sometimes called the "fear imprint period," because during this age, anything negative that happens to the puppy may have the potential to affect him for life. This critical time period may be when you first obtain your puppy, so it is very important to

Fun Facts

Although your Sheltie may *seem* to understand everything you say, he really understands only certain words and phrases, and he does not understand conversations. The "average" dog is reportedly capable of learning and understanding about 160 words (Coren, 2006) and Shelties are much smarter than the "average" dog. The scientific journal *Behavioral Processes* published a study in 2010 in which a Border Collie named Chaser learned 1,022 nouns within a three-year period. She also learned several commands and has, to date, the largest vocabulary of any known dog. The scientists believed Chaser was capable of learning more words, but they simply ran out of time to continue teaching her. Based on this fascinating study, it seems quite possible that a well-trained Shetland Sheepdog could learn and remember several hundred words throughout his lifetime.

focus on building your Sheltie's confidence. Make sure he has lots of experiences—and that all of his experiences are good ones! If your Sheltie acts frightened, behave calmly so he knows there is nothing to fear. Your puppy will take his cues from you. When he is uncertain, encourage him to explore and praise him for his courage. Do not reinforce or reward fear behavior. Instead, speak to your puppy calmly (or enthusiastically and playfully, depending on the circumstance) and continue to gradually introduce him to different people, places, things, environments, and situations.

Always praise your Shetland Sheepdog for his confident, outgoing, good behavior. Make socialization a fun game—for life!

Communicating with Your Sheltie

Shetland Sheepdogs rank among the most intelligent of dog breeds. In one study assessing trainability, the Shetland Sheepdog was ranked third most trainable out of 56 breeds surveyed. In another study comparing 110 different breeds, the Shetland Sheepdog ranked sixth in trainability. Clearly, Shelties pay close attention to their people and are skilled at communicating, understanding, and responding.

When you think about communication and responses, try to think about it from your Sheltie's point of view. He relies heavily on your facial expressions, postural cues, body and hand movements, and voice and intonations to try to understand you. Try not to send your Sheltie mixed messages that can confuse him. Miscommunication leads to misunderstanding and unwanted responses. If you are consistent and always use the same words and intonations for the same things, your Sheltie will learn words and phrases very quickly.

Voice

Your Sheltie hears your voice continually and *listens intently*. He relies on the intonation and volume of your voice to know your mood. Your voice tells your pet if you are pleased with him, happy to see him, calm and relaxed, or angry, frightened, or sad. The way you speak, together with your actions, help your Sheltie associate words and behaviors. For example, if you always say, "Let's go for a ride" and jingle your car keys, or if you always say, "Go for a walk" when you reach for the leash, your Sheltie will quickly learn what you mean through a consistent combination of voice, words, phrases, and actions. If you are consistent, calm, and clear when you communicate with your Sheltie, he will surprise you with his learning ability, word knowledge, and memory retention.

Hands

Hands are one of your greatest tools for communicating with your Sheltie. Shelties are very attentive to hand movements and quickly learn hand signals (see Chapter 7, "Training and Activities"). From the first time you hold your Sheltie, you communicate friendship and affection to him. You use your hands to feed him meals and treats, to bathe and groom him, to play games, and to caress and praise him. Your hands also give your Sheltie additional olfactory information about you when you are near him. For example, he can smell the soap you used to wash your hands, or knows you have just handled food, or can tell if you have just petted the cat. Hands can be very useful for continuing communication with your Sheltie when he is an old dog. If his hearing starts to fail, you can still give your Sheltie important commands by hand. For example, if he cannot hear a moving car in the driveway, you can signal him to *sit* and *stay* in a safe spot. Hands are very important!

Facial Expressions

Shelties are highly tuned in to their owner's moods and emotions and are very good at reading their owner's facial expressions. Elaborate research studies have shown that dogs have discrimination capabilities when inspecting human faces and can use facial cues alone to differentiate individual humans.

Body Movement

Body movement and body language are excellent ways of communicating with your Sheltie. Body movements are closely linked to hand movements, and your Sheltie cues off of your movements to have a sense of your moods and intentions. Bending down or lowering your body can indicate play behavior; lunging forward can appear aggressive. Something as simple as turning away from your Sheltie and ignoring him can be a clear message that he made a mistake and you are displeased. Shelties hate to be ignored!

Chapter Six

Health and Nutrition

The best health care you can give your Sheltie is *preventive* health care and good nutrition. It is easier to prevent health problems than it is to treat or cure them. Also, many health problems are caused by a poor or unbalanced diet.

Regular health checkups are important. Your veterinarian can detect health problems that may not yet be obvious and treat them before they become serious. Shelties are very stoic and can sometimes hide signs that something is wrong until the problem has significantly progressed. The sooner a health problem is detected and treated, the better the chances are for your Sheltie to make a rapid, full recovery.

It is easy to tell when your Sheltie is feeling great. He is bright-eyed, alert, and eager to join you in a game or outing. If your Sheltie is not acting normally, seems depressed, is not eating or drinking, is not urinating or defecating, is lethargic, is losing weight, or has any other problems, it is time to call your veterinarian.

Is Your Shetland Sheepdog Healthy?

Check your Sheltie daily, from his nose to his toes, as you play with him. Your pet's overall demeanor should be alert and happy, even enthusiastic. His body should be well proportioned, with good muscle tone, and not too thin or too heavy. Your Sheltie's full coat can be deceiving and make him look heavier than he really is. Weigh your Sheltie once a week, so you will know if he loses or gains weight. When you feel through the coat, you should be able to feel the ribs slightly, but they should not protrude, and your dog should not feel bony.

Your Sheltie should stand normally on all four feet, without favoring a limb or limping. His posture should be correct and relaxed. A hunched-up posture can mean back or abdominal pain. A drooping head may indicate neck, chest, or front-limb pain. A head tilt suggests ear pain, ear infection, parasites, or a nervous system problem.

Eyes and Nose Your Sheltie's nose should be free of discharge. A cold, wet nose is normal, but a dry nose does *not* indicate illness. His eyes should be bright, clear, and free of discharge. Call your veterinarian if you observe squinting or redness; infection (yellow or green discharge) in or around your pet's eyes; or if the colored part of the eye (iris), or the surface of the eye (cornea), appears cloudy or hazy. Eye problems, such as injury or infection, can be very painful, interfere with tear production, and require special medications. If not treated immediately, some eye problems can lead to loss of vision.

Shelties can inherit eye disorders, such as choroidal hypoplasia (also called Collie eye anomaly [CEA] or Sheltie eye syndrome [SES]), progressive retinal atrophy (PRA), and corneal dystrophy (see Chapter 10, "Special Considerations").

Mouth Your Sheltie's gums should be healthy and bright pink, and his teeth should be free of plaque buildup. Check for swollen gums or dental problems such as retained deciduous (baby) teeth, missing teeth, incorrectly positioned teeth that protrude into the gums, abnormal dental occlusions, and cracked or broken teeth.

A Sheltie puppy has 28 deciduous teeth: 12 incisors, 4 canine teeth, and 12 premolars.

An adult Sheltie has 42 teeth: 12 incisors, 4 canine teeth, 16 premolars, and 10 molars.

The baby (deciduous) teeth start erupting at about three to four weeks of age (but not all at once) and, depending on the type of tooth, will fall out between two and seven months of age as the adult teeth eventually replace them.

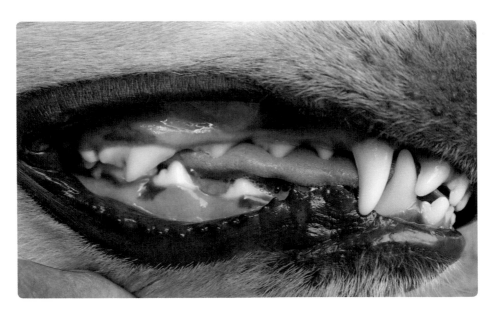

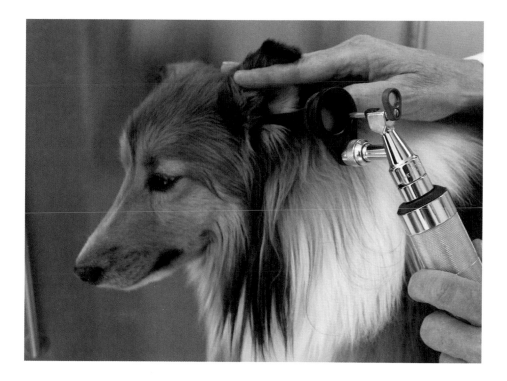

Ears Clean your Sheltie's ears regularly and check for dirt and wax buildup. If your Sheltie's ears are sensitive, painful, or reddened; if they have a foul odor or discharge; or if he shakes his head and scratches at his ears, contact your veterinarian right away. Your Sheltie could have an ear infection or parasites (such as mites or fleas), or a foreign object (such as a grass awn) in his ear(s).

Ear problems can lead to severe, permanent hearing impairment if they are not treated.

Skin and Coat Brush your Sheltie's coat at least once weekly, or more often as needed, to keep his coat well groomed and beautiful. Your pet's skin should be healthy and free of parasites, such as fleas, ticks, and mange mites. His skin should not be dry, flaky, or greasy.

CAUTION

Keep your Sheltie clean and well groomed at all times. If your Sheltie's hair is matted or contaminated with urine or fecal material, especially under the tail, flies can lay hundreds of eggs in the matted hair. Maggots develop quickly in the damp, filthy, matted hair and rapidly invade, infect, and destroy body tissues.

It is normal for your Sheltie to shed out his old coat seasonally (this is called "blowing coat") as he grows a new coat, but if your pet sheds excessively all the time, or if his skin doesn't look healthy, consult your veterinarian.

CHECKLIST

Health Problems

Contact your veterinarian immediately if your Sheltie has any of the following problems:

- ✔ Fever
- ✔ Pain
- ✔ Loss of appetite
- ✔ Lethargy
- ✔ Vomiting
- ✔ Diarrhea
- ✔ Discharge from the eyes
- ✔ Breathing problems or difficulty
- ✔ Coughing
- ✔ Choking
- ✔ Lameness

- ✔ Head-shaking
- ✔ Trembling
- ✔ Blood in the urine or feces
- ✔ Inability to urinate
- ✔ Vaginal discharge
- ✔ Severe constipation or inability to have a bowel movement
- ✔ Seizures
- ✔ Dehydration
- ✔ Weight loss
- ✔ Bloating

Legs and Feet Legs and feet should be pain-free. Lameness can be difficult to detect if there is lameness in more than one limb. Lameness can be caused by injury; bone and joint, muscular, or nervous system problems; a cut footpad; or a foreign object. Feel the hind limbs. Bones that slip or pop may indicate patellar luxation (slipped kneecap).

Check all four feet and between the toes for thorns and grass awns that cause pain and infection when hidden in the hair or tissues. Check the nail beds for redness and infection, and check for torn toe nails and overgrown nails. Trim nails regularly so they do not grow into the tissues of the foot-pads, causing pain, infection, and lameness. If your Sheltie has dewclaws (the small nails high on the inside of the front feet), be sure to trim these. Dewclaws can catch on anything from the underbrush to indoor carpeting. When they get snagged, there is often bleeding and tissue damage. Untrimmed dewclaws may spiral as they grow, and burrow into the foot and cause pain. Many breeders have their puppies' dewclaws removed at three days of age.

Gait Your Sheltie should walk, trot, and run with ease and flowing movement. He should not limp or have difficulty moving.

Helpful Hints

Feel your Sheltie's body to be sure he is not too thin. All that hair can make him look bigger than he really is! You should be able to feel your Sheltie's ribs slightly, but they should not protrude, feel bony, or be visible. The ribs should have a nice layer of flesh over them, but not a thick layer of fat.

HOME BASICS
How to Check Your Sheltie's Vital Signs

Pulse: Place your fingers between your dog's ribs on the left side of the chest, behind the elbow, and feel the heartbeat, or place your fingers on the inside middle portion of either upper thigh, or in the groin area. *Normal resting pulse is 80 to 180 beats per minute, depending on whether your Sheltie is at rest or has been active.*

Temperature: Take your Sheltie's temperature rectally with a digital thermometer. Lubricate the tip of the thermometer and gently insert it about 1 inch (2.5 cm) into your pet's rectum. *Normal Sheltie body temperature ranges from 100.5 to 102.5°F (38–39°C).*

Circulation: Capillary refill time (CRT) is a good indicator of circulation. Press on the gums for a second with your finger and then release. The gums will blanch and then should return to a bright pink color as blood returns to the tissues (capillaries refill). *Normal CRT is 2 seconds or less.*

Respiration rate: Count the number of breaths your Sheltie takes in one minute. Respiration rate increases with excitement, heat, difficulty breathing, or panting.
Normal respiration is 15 to 30 breaths per minute.

Hydration: Lift the skin over the shoulders and let go. The skin returns to place in a sufficiently hydrated animal. If the skin is slow to return, or remains "tented," then your Sheltie is dehydrated and needs fluids.

Under the Tail Check under the tail for signs of problems, such as swelling, hernias, anal sac impaction, abscesses, cysts, inflammation, fecal matter, mats, and parasites. Keep the hair under the tail clean and well brushed.

Sexual Maturity If your Sheltie is a female and has not been spayed, check her regularly for vaginal discharge, signs of estrus, or signs of infection. If you have an intact male (not neutered), both of his testicles should be fully descended into the scrotum. One or both retained testicles (cryptorchidism) is believed to be an inherited problem. The retained testicle(s) must be surgically removed or it can develop tumors (cancer) in later life. Retained testicles do not produce sperm and are usually abnormal in appearance.

Your Sheltie is a lucky dog! He lives in a time when most canine health problems and diseases can be prevented or treated. Malnutrition, severe parasitism, and bacterial and viral diseases used to be common canine killers. Dogs today benefit greatly from the superior nutrition offered in specially formulated and balanced diets and from excellent veterinary care.

Choosing a Veterinarian

Here are some guidelines to help you select the right veterinarian for your Sheltie.

- Ideally, choose a veterinarian who knows a lot about Shelties and shares your enthusiasm for the breed. Ask the breeder, other Sheltie owners, dog trainers, groomers, and members of your local kennel club which veterinarians they recommend.
- Ask your friends and neighbors for recommendation of a veterinarian in whom they have confidence.
- Visit veterinary hospitals in your area. Meet the doctors and staff. Tour the facility.
- Inquire about the education, experience, and training of the veterinarians and veterinary staff.
- Find a veterinary practice near you with convenient hours. Ideally, it should offer 24-hour emergency service.

Helpful Hints

Choose a veterinarian who is familiar with Shelties. Find a veterinarian *before* you need one and before a possible emergency situation. Take a test drive to the hospital so you know where to find it in advance of an emergency.

FYI: Common Tests and Procedures

Test	Purpose	Procedures	Purpose
Fecal Test	Check for internal parasites: worms, protozoa	Vaccinations	Provide immunity against common canine viral and bacterial diseases
Heartworm Test	Check blood for heartworm disease	Microchip Identification	Permanent form of identification in case your Sheltie is lost
Complete blood test and serum chemistries	Check blood for signs of anemia or infection, and check organ function and other body functions	Neuter	Surgery to remove reproductive organs to prevent reproduction and some kinds of cancer
Skin scraping	Check for skin mites	Deworming (vermifuge)	Treatment to eliminate internal parasites (worms)
Fungal culture	Check for fungi, such as ringworm	Dewclaw removal	Surgical removal of small "thumb claw" on inside of front legs
Bacterial culture and sensitivity	Identify bacterial species and best antibiotic to treat the infection	Physical examination	Ensure and monitor health

Vaccinations

Vaccinations (inoculations, immunizations) are the best method currently available to protect your Sheltie against serious, life-threatening diseases to which he may be exposed. Although there is not a vaccine available for every known canine disease, vaccines are available for some of the most common and deadly ones. Your veterinarian will customize your Sheltie's vaccine recommendations and schedule according to his lifestyle, age, health condition, past medical history, and risk of exposure.

Helpful Hints

Pet Health Insurance

The American Kennel Club offers a health insurance program. Your veterinarian can also recommend a pet health-care insurance program that is right for your Shetland Sheepdog.

BE PREPARED! Common Canine Diseases That Can Be Prevented by Immunizations

Disease	Cause	Spread	Contagion	Signs
Distemper	Viral	Airborne, body excretions	Highly contagious, especially among young dogs	Difficulty breathing, coughing, discharge from nose and eyes, vomiting, diarrhea, dehydration, trembling, blindness, paralysis, seizures
Parvovirus	Viral	Contaminated feces	Highly contagious, especially among puppies	Diarrhea, dehydration, vomiting, heart problems and heart failure
Infectious canine hepatitis	Viral	Body excretions, urine	Highly contagious, especially among puppies and young dogs	Liver inflammation, jaundice, "blue eye" caused by fluid buildup; kidney damage, pain, internal bleeding
Leptospirosis	Bacterial	Urine contaminated in kennels or from wild animals	Highly contagious	Kidney and liver damage, jaundice, kidney failure, internal bleeding, anemia
Parainfluenza Bordetellosis Both cause "kennel cough."	Viral Bacterial	Airborne, sneeze and cough droplets	Highly contagious, especially in boarding kennels	Dry, hacking, persistent cough; may cause permanent damage to airways
Lyme disease	Bacterial	Spread by the bite of an infected tick or contaminated body fluids		Swollen lymph nodes, lethargy, loss of appetite, joint swelling, lameness, heart and kidney disease
Rabies	Viral	Saliva (bite wounds)		Fatal, preceded by nervous system signs including paralysis, incoordination, and change in behavior

The American Animal Hospital Association Canine Vaccine Guidelines assigns vaccines into three categories:

Core Vaccines Recommended	Canine parvovirus Canine distemper Canine adenovirus-2 (hepatitis) Rabies
Non-Core Vaccines Optional, depending on the dog's location and risk of exposure	Parainfluenza *Bordetella bronchiceptica* (kennel cough) *Borrelia burgdorferi* (Lyme disease) *Leptospira*
Not recommended	Canine coronavirus *Giardia lambia*

Treatments

Viral infections: There is no treatment to kill a virus once infection has occurred. Treatment consists of supportive therapy such as fluids, antibiotics to control secondary bacterial infection, medications, and rest.

Rabies virus: The rabies virus is fatal to dogs and other mammals. A post-exposure treatment exists for humans infected with the rabies virus, but there is not one for animals.

Bacterial infections: Bacterial infections are treated with antibiotics and supportive therapy.

Parasite Control

Dogs can become infested with several kinds of external parasites. Check your Sheltie for fleas and ticks after every outing, especially during the summer months, and keep his coat brushed and well groomed. The number one cause of scratching and hair loss in dogs is caused by flea infestations.

Internal parasites (roundworms, hookworms, whipworms, tapeworms, and heartworms) and external parasites (fleas, ticks, ear mites, and mange-causing mites) can be killed and controlled with prescription medications available as once-a-month tablets, topical applications, or by injection.

Important! Many Shelties (and other herding breeds) carry a gene called the Multiple Drug Resistance (MDR1) gene. This gene makes Shelties more sensitive to certain medications, including some that are used in some parasite-control products (see Chapter 10, "Special Considerations").

Discuss drug sensitivity with your veterinarian. New products for parasite control are being released continually. Ask your veterinarian which antiparasitic drugs are safe for your Sheltie and which may pose a risk for him if he carries the MDR1 gene. There is a DNA test available, so ask your veterinarian to test your Sheltie to find out if he carries the MDR1 gene.

First Aid for Your Sheltie

The difference between life and death for your Sheltie could depend on how prepared you are. Prepare an emergency kit for your dog today! Put all your supplies together now so you do not waste precious time trying to find what you need if there is an emergency.

- Write down the doses for different medications, and put the list in the kit so you can give the medicine without having to calculate the dose in the middle of a crisis.
- Make a copy of the emergency instructions in this book and put it in your first aid kit for easy reference.
- Keep the poison control center phone number in the first aid kit.
- Put the kit in a special place. Make sure the pet sitter knows where the kit is.
- When you travel with your Sheltie, take the first aid kit with you.

FYI: Parasites That Affect Shelties

Parasites	Transmission to Dogs	Transmission to Humans	Prevention
Internal			
Roundworms	Ingestion of eggs in feces of infected animals; transmitted from mother to pup *in utero*, or in the milk	Accidental ingestion of eggs from contact with infected fecal material	Some parasiticides may be given to very young pups. Dewormings should be repeated as needed.
Hookworms	Ingestion of larvae in feces of infected animals, direct skin contact with larvae	Direct skin contact with larvae in soil con-taminated with feces of infected animals, acci-dental ingestion of larvae	Parasiticides
Whipworms	Contact with feces	No	Parasiticides
Tapeworms	Contact with fleas and feces, ingestion of fleas, eating raw meat (wild rodents)	Accidental ingestion of fleas and larvae	Parasiticides
Heartworms	Mosquito bite	No	Parasiticides
Protozoa	Contact with feces	Accidental ingestion of organisms in fecal material	Parasiticides
External			
Fleas	Allergy to flea saliva, skin irritation and itch-ing, hair loss, transmis-sion of tapeworms	Fleas may bite humans. Tapeworms also may be indirectly transmitted to people.	
Ticks	Transmission of Lyme disease, skin irritation and infection, tick paralysis	Humans can contract Lyme disease from direct contact with ticks.	Always wear gloves when removing ticks from your dog.
Sarcoptic mange	Skin lesions and itching, hair loss	Sarcoptic mange can spread from pets to people by contract.	
Demodectic mange	Skin lesions, localized or generalized hair loss	No	

Emergency ABCs: Airway, Breathing, Circulation

The first and most important things to check for on your Sheltie in an emergency are as follows:

1. **Airway: Open, unobstructed airway (trachea)**
   Open your Sheltie's mouth widely to see if anything is blocking the air passageway. Use a penlight or flashlight to look down the throat to check for foreign objects that could obstruct the trachea, such as food, toy particles, bones, sticks, or pebbles. If possible, remove the object immediately to prevent suffocation. A short wooden dowel 2–3 inches (5–8 cm) in diameter can be carefully inserted between the back molars to hold the mouth open while you try to remove the object. You may have to use forceps, if available. Do not push the object farther down the throat with your fingers.

2. **Breathing**
   If your Sheltie is not breathing, open his mouth, remove any objects or debris, and clear away secretions. Pull his tongue out straight so it does not block the throat. Place your mouth over your pet's nose and muzzle so that it makes a tight seal and blow gently, just enough to make the chest rise. Do not blow too hard or you can damage your dog's lungs. Release so air can be expelled. Repeat this procedure every five seconds until your Sheltie breathes on his own.

   Check gum color often. If your Sheltie is receiving enough oxygen, his gums should return to a bright pink color.

   Be careful! Do not attempt this procedure if your Sheltie is conscious, or you may be bitten!

3. Cardiac: Beating Heart

If you cannot feel your Sheltie's pulse, or cannot hear his heart beat when you place your ear against his chest, begin cardiopulmonary resuscitation (CPR) immediately. Place your pet on his right side. Place one hand on top of the other and gently press your fingers on the left side of your Sheltie's chest, slightly above and directly behind the elbow. Continue to press and release at a rate of one to two presses every one to two seconds. Remember to also breathe into the nostrils every five seconds. Continue CPR until your Sheltie is able to breathe on his own and you can feel his pulse.

Be sure to take your Sheltie to a veterinarian for treatment immediately after you have resuscitated him. He will need follow-up emergency care to ensure that he does not relapse.

Emergency Treatments

Important: If your Sheltie is suffering from any of the problems listed, consult your veterinarian immediately. This section is for emergency first aid only and is not a substitute for veterinary care.

Bite Wounds Wounds to the head, neck, chest, and abdomen are serious. Wounds that penetrate the body cavity are life-threatening, especially if the lungs are partially collapsed or the internal organs are exposed.

If body organs are exposed, cover them with a warm, sterile, damp saline dressing. Do not push the organs back into the body. Rush your Sheltie to a veterinary hospital.

For bite wounds, lacerations, tears, and puncture wounds, cleanse them well with a wound-disinfectant solution. Antibiotics and sutures may be required. Consult your veterinarian.

Contact your veterinarian immediately about bite wounds, and discuss the possible risk of rabies.

Bleeding or Hemorrhage Excessive bleeding and pale gums indicate severe blood loss, which is life-threatening. Use gauze or a clean towel compress to apply firm pressure over the wound to stop the bleeding. If a large blood vessel in a limb has been severed, apply a tourniquet above the cut area. Loosen the tourniquet every 10 minutes to relieve pressure and allow circulation while your Sheltie is being transported to an emergency hospital.

Bone Fractures Symptoms of bone fractures include swelling, pain, tenderness, abnormal limb position or movement, limping, and crepitation ("crunching" sound or vibration when touched

CAUTION

Dogs behave unpredictably when they are in pain or frightened. *For your safety and your Sheltie's safety, always muzzle your pet before initiating emergency treatment.* You can make a muzzle from a strip of soft cotton cloth, or gauze, about 18 inches (46 cm) long and 2 inches (5 cm) wide. Wrap the gauze around your Sheltie's muzzle, as close to the face as possible, and tie it securely under the chin. Take the ends of the gauze and tie them behind the head.

Do not muzzle your Sheltie if he is not breathing or is unconscious.

or moved). Bone may remain under the skin or protrude through it.

If the bone is exposed, do not try to replace or cleanse it. Stop the bleeding and cover the wound with a sterile bandage to prevent further wound contamination. Place your Sheltie on a soft bed, keep him calm and warm, and restrict his activity while you transport him to a veterinary hospital.

Burns Signs of burns include pain, and red, swollen, inflamed, and blistered skin.

Thermal and electrical burns: Apply a cold, wet cloth or a cold pack to the area to cool the burn. Protect the burned area from the air with an ointment, such as Neosporin.

Chemical burns: Flush the burn profusely with water or saline to rinse the caustic chemical from the area. Prevent your Sheltie from licking the area or he will swallow the caustic substance and burn his mouth and esophagus.

Choking (Refer to "Airway")

Cuts Clip hair from around the cut, clean the cut well with mild soap and water, dry the area, and apply antibiotic ointment. Bandage the wound (not too tightly) to keep it clean. *Change the bandage daily.*

Eye Injuries Eye injuries can be very painful. Symptoms include squinting, tearing, sensitivity to light, redness, swelling, and dilated pupils. If the eyes require flushing, use a commercial, gentle, safe eyewash solution. Place your Sheltie in an area with subdued light. Contact your veterinarian immediately to increase chances of saving the eye(s) and vision and for pain relief.

Dehydration

To test for dehydration, pull up the skin at the nape of the neck. If it does not quickly return to normal position and remains "tented," your Sheltie is dehydrated. Offer water only if he is conscious and able to drink. Do not force water if he is unconscious or too weak to drink, or he may aspirate the water into his lungs. Consult your veterinarian immediately, as your Sheltie may need intravenous fluid therapy.

Heatstroke

Shelties carry heavy coats, so it is easy for them to become overheated and suffer from heatstroke. Symptoms include frantic, rapid breathing; bright

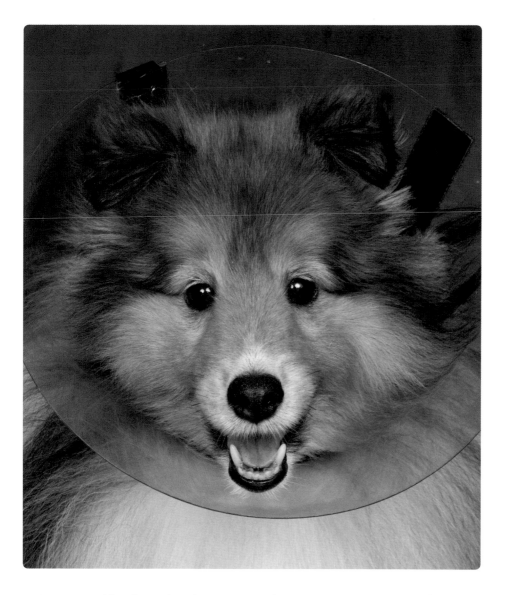

red gums and bright red curling tongue; thick drool; vomiting; diarrhea; dehydration; and a rectal temperature of 104°F (40°C) or higher. Heatstroke progresses rapidly, and as it does, the body organs become affected, and the animal weakens, goes into shock, and then a coma, and dies. All of this can occur within a few minutes.

Act quickly to lower your Sheltie's body temperature by wetting him repeatedly with cool (not cold) water. Check his body temperature every three to five minutes. When the temperature has dropped to 102°F (39°C), stop wetting, and monitor your Sheltie closely. When your Sheltie is conscious, offer him water. Take him to your veterinarian immediately for

CHECKLIST

Supplies for Your First Aid Kit

The basic supplies and materials you need for your Sheltie's first aid kit can be purchased at your local pharmacy or from your veterinarian.

- ✔ Bandage scissors
- ✔ Small, regular, blunt-tipped scissors
- ✔ Thermometer
- ✔ Tourniquet (a strip of gauze will work)
- ✔ Tweezers
- ✔ Forceps
- ✔ Mouth gag (small wooden dowel will work)
- ✔ Hydrogen peroxide 3 percent solution
- ✔ Triple antibiotic ointment
- ✔ Roll of gauze bandage
- ✔ Sterile gauze pads, 4 by 4 inches (10 by 10 cm)
- ✔ Telfa no-stick pads
- ✔ Sterile dressing and compresses
- ✔ Sterile physiologic saline solution
- ✔ Elastic bandage (waterproof)
- ✔ Bandage tape (waterproof)
- ✔ Self-adhesive bandage (VetWrap type)
- ✔ Activated charcoal (for treatment of poisoning)
- ✔ Eyewash (sterile physiologic saline will work)

- ✔ Antihistamine capsules or tablets (diphenhydramine or chlorpheneramine)
- ✔ Antihistamine cream (diphenhydramine)
- ✔ Ophthalmic ointment (should *not* contain hydrocortisone)
- ✔ Cold compress (instant cold type)
- ✔ Muzzle (comfortable nylon)
- ✔ Blanket
- ✔ Cotton towels
- ✔ Paper towels
- ✔ Disinfectant soap
- ✔ Sponge
- ✔ Exam gloves (vinyl)
- ✔ Penlight and/or flashlight
- ✔ Bottled water
- ✔ Electrolyte solution, such as Pedialyte
- ✔ Nutrical or other high-sugar product, such as Karo syrup (corn syrup)
- ✔ Plastic bags
- ✔ Clippers (to shave wound areas)
- ✔ Feeding syringes

follow-up care. Intravenous fluids and medications will be needed to treat shock and prevent cerebral edema (brain swelling).

Hypoglycemia (Low Blood Sugar)

Low blood sugar in puppies and dogs can be caused by many things, including not eating enough food, disease, and some artificial sweeteners (such as xylitol, found in sugar-free gum and candy). As blood sugar drops, the dog becomes drowsy, lethargic, weak, uncoordinated, unable to walk, and finally unconscious. Gums are pale and pupils are dilated.

Rub a sugar-rich substance on your Sheltie's gums, such as corn syrup, or Nutrical. Keep your Sheltie warm and rush him to a veterinary hospital.

FYI: Check Your Sheltie's Gums

You can learn a lot about your Sheltie's health by checking his gums.

- Bright pink: normal
- Red: inflammation, fever, heatstroke, possible poisoning
- Red specks or red spots: bleeding problems or infection
- Pale pink or white: anemia, hemorrhage, or significant blood loss
- Blue, gray: insufficient oxygen delivery to the body
- Yellow: jaundice (icterus), liver problems
- "Muddy" gray, brown: very serious, near death in many cases
- "Tacky" or sticky to the touch: dehydrated

To save time in an emergency, ask a friend or family member to call the veterinary emergency hospital in advance to let the staff know you are on your way with your pet and to describe the emergency situation. This gives the veterinarians and staff more time to prepare so they are ready to help you and your Sheltie the moment you arrive.

Hypothermia

Low body temperature is most commonly a problem with very young puppies. Symptoms include shivering, lethargy, slow heart rate, slow respiration, coma, and death.

Warm your Sheltie *slowly*! Wrap him in a blanket. Fill plastic water bottles with warm (*not hot*) water, and place the bottles near but not directly against his body. Leave his head exposed and watch him closely. *Do not use an electric heating pad*. Check your Sheltie's body temperature every five minutes and do not let it rise above 101.5°F (39°C). Take your Sheltie to a veterinary hospital for follow-up care.

Insect Stings

Insect stings cause swelling, redness, pain, and itching. A severe allergic reaction can result in sensitive individuals, leading to facial and throat swelling, difficulty breathing, vomiting, and unconsciousness.

Bee stings: Remove the stinger quickly. Do not squeeze the bulb attached to the stinger because it can increase the amount of venom injected.

Apply a paste of water and baking soda or an ice pack to the sting to relieve pain.

Wasp and hornet stings: Apply vinegar to the area for pain relief.

Helpful Hints

Bee stingers are barbed and left in the skin. Wasps, hornets, and yellow jackets do not leave stingers in the skin.

Antihistamine creams applied topically to the area, or antihistamines, especially diphenyhydramine hydrochloride (Benadryl or its generic equivalent) taken by mouth, may be beneficial. Over-the-counter topical pain relievers for insect stings are available.

Poisoning

Symptoms of poisoning vary according to the toxin. They include restlessness, drooling, abdominal pain, vomiting, diarrhea, unconsciousness, seizures, shock, and death. Contact the poison control center and your veterinarian immediately. If you know what poison your Sheltie consumed and you have the container for it, read the label and follow the emergency instructions for treatment. To induce vomiting, give ¼ to ½ teaspoon of 3 percent hydrogen peroxide. Use activated charcoal (available in powder, tablet, or capsule form from your veterinarian) to dilute and absorb ingested poisons. All poisonings require veterinary care.

FYI: The 10 Most Common Poisonings in Dogs

1. Human medications: prescription drugs, ibuprofen, thyroxin, pseudoephedrine
2. Insecticides: ant and roach baits, bug sprays
3. Rodenticides: rat, mouse, gopher bait
4. Human foods: chocolate, grapes, raisins, macadamia nuts, artificial sweetener xylitol, nutmeg, coffee, tea
5. Veterinary medications: accidental overdoses
6. Household toxins and cleaning products, such as bleach, pool chemicals
7. Poisonous plants
8. Antifreeze
9. Yard products: fertilizers
10. Chemicals: hydrocarbons in paint, varnish, furniture polish

Seizures

Seizures may be mild or severe, ranging from a tremor of short duration, to violent convulsions, chomping jaws, frothing at the mouth, stiffening of the neck and limbs, and cessation of breathing.

During a severe seizure the animal is not conscious and can be hurt thrashing about on the floor. Try to prevent your pet from being injured. Your Sheltie may appear to be choking, but do not handle his mouth or you will be bitten. After the seizure has ended, your Sheltie will be disoriented and exhausted. Take him to your veterinarian immediately for follow-up care.

Shock

Shock occurs when there is a decreased blood supply to the body's organs. Symptoms include vomiting, diarrhea, weakness, difficulty breathing, increased heart rate, collapse, and coma.

Shock leads to rapid death unless immediate veterinary care is given, including fluid and oxygen therapy and a variety of medications, as needed.

Helpful Hints

Dog Food Ingredients

You cannot rely entirely on the comparison of ingredient labels to select dog food for your Sheltie!

- Ingredients include *everything* that is mixed together to make a specific dog food.
- Dog food labels list ingredients in decreasing order of preponderance by weight, but they do not tell you about the ingredients' quality or digestibility.
- Ingredients can be nutritional (protein, carbohydrates, fat, vitamins, minerals) or non-nutritional (food additives, artificial coloring, artificial flavorings, food preservatives).

Sheltie Nutrition

High-quality nutrition is an essential part of keeping your Sheltie in excellent health. The food you feed your Sheltie will strongly affect his health, development, coat quality, mental acuity, life span, and overall well-being. A large number of canine health problems are linked to an unbalanced diet, inadequate nutrition, or the wrong kinds of foods. Always feed your Sheltie the best food you possibly can.

Your Sheltie's diet will need to be adjusted throughout his life. For example, when he is a puppy, he will need a food that provides complete and balanced nutrition for puppy growth and development. As he reaches adolescence, his diet will change based on his growth rate, activity level, metabolism, coat growth, environment, and genetics.

When your Sheltie is an adult, his caloric requirement may increase if he is very active working on a ranch herding; competing in agility, herding,

or other canine events; or under stress on the show circuit. Female Shelties that are pregnant or lactating may easily need more than twice their normal caloric intake, depending on their condition and the size of the litter. If your Sheltie is old, or recovering from an illness, he will need a diet based on his health condition and special needs. Some medical conditions call for special prescription diets.

Shelties were not bred to be sedentary dogs. Inactive dogs need fewer calories than working dogs do, but they still enjoy eating! Unfortunately, if they are fed too much for their activity level, they become overweight. For these animals, prescription weight-reduction diets are sometimes necessary (along with a reasonable exercise program!) to help them maintain a healthy weight.

Clearly, what to feed and how much are not the same for every dog, and dietary requirements change throughout a dog's life. As your Sheltie grows and ages, consult your veterinarian to learn which type of dog food would be most beneficial for him and how much to feed him based on his health, age, and activity level at that time.

Nutrients

Nutrients are necessary for life's processes. Some are energy producing (sugars, amino acids, fatty acids), and some do not produce energy but are required for life (water, oxygen, vitamins, minerals). The type and amount of nutrients in a dog food mixture make up the nutrient profile.

The American Association of Feed Control Officials (AAFCO) requires dog food companies to demonstrate the nutritional adequacy of their food by feeding trials or by meeting the AAFCO Nutrient Profile and to make a statement about nutritional adequacy on all of their products (except treats and snacks) such as "complete and balanced nutrition."

Proteins

Proteins and protein quality are the most important health factors in your Sheltie's diet. Proteins come from plant and animal sources. Animal-source protein is better for dogs because it provides

Helpful Hints

Do not give your Sheltie

- any medications prescribed for you or for your other pets, or
- home-made sugar or salt mixtures.

Check with your veterinarian about the dose and safety of any medication before giving it to your Sheltie.

FYI: "Foods" That Are Toxic to Dogs

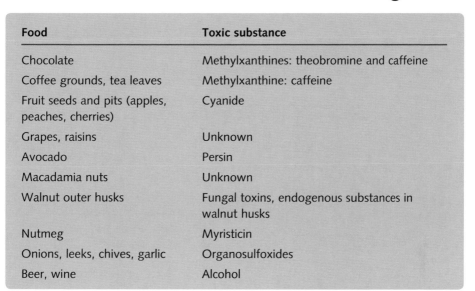

Food	Toxic substance
Chocolate	Methylxanthines: theobromine and caffeine
Coffee grounds, tea leaves	Methylxanthine: caffeine
Fruit seeds and pits (apples, peaches, cherries)	Cyanide
Grapes, raisins	Unknown
Avocado	Persin
Macadamia nuts	Unknown
Walnut outer husks	Fungal toxins, endogenous substances in walnut husks
Nutmeg	Myristicin
Onions, leeks, chives, garlic	Organosulfoxides
Beer, wine	Alcohol

the essential amino acids dogs need, in the correct balance. Animal-source protein includes beef, chicken, turkey, duck, lamb, fish, and eggs.

Fats

Fats are an important part of your pet's diet and necessary for healthy skin and a beautiful coat. There are several kinds of fats—animal fats, vegetable oils, olive oil, fish oils—and all have different effects on the body. Fats add flavor to food, provide energy, and are important for the absorption and assimilation of fat-soluble vitamins A, D, E, and K.

Carbohydrates

Carbohydrates are sugars, starches, and fibers. *Researchers have not yet determined the exact amount of carbohydrates needed in the canine diet, yet carbohydrates make up the major portion of today's commercial dog foods because they are an inexpensive source of energy.*

Rice or a combination of wholesome grains as a carbohydrate source are better for your dog than diets containing corn. Dog foods with corn or corn-

Helpful Hints

Check food labels for high-quality protein sources. Whenever possible, select foods that indicate "meat" is the key ingredient, rather than "by-products."

- Meat: muscle and skin, with or without bone
- Meal: protein source ground into particles
- By-products: heads, feet, guts, bone

FYI: Food Additives

Additives are non-nutritional chemicals added to the food to enhance color, flavor, and texture, to extend shelf life, to prevent food from becoming rancid, or to slow down bacterial or fungal growth. Chemicals added to make dog food more colorful are targeted at impressing the consumers. Dogs do not see colors the way people do and are interested only in the way the food *smells*. Your Sheltie sees red as a dark gray color. That red food coloring in your pet's food was added to make *you* think it looks meaty. It doesn't fool your Sheltie, and if it doesn't pass his smell test, he won't eat it!

meal as a source of carbohydrates can cause food and skin allergies. Fiber is used in many weight-reduction diets because dogs cannot digest fiber.

Vitamins

Fat-soluble vitamins are A, D, E, and K. Water-soluble vitamins are all of the B vitamins and vitamin C. Unlike humans, dogs make their own vitamin C and do not need it supplemented in their diet.

Minerals

Minerals are required for skeletal growth and development, and muscle and nerve function. Minerals necessary for life include calcium, phosphorus, sodium, potassium, magnesium, zinc, selenium, iron, manganese, copper, and iodine.

Obesity

Overeating is the most common cause of obesity in dogs. Obesity is a form of malnutrition in which there is a ratio of too much fat to lean body tissue. The best way to prevent your Sheltie from becoming overweight is to not overfeed him and to make sure he has enough exercise.

Water

Water is the most important of all nutrients. Dogs may be able to survive several days without food, but a dog cannot survive for long without water. It is very important that your Sheltie has plenty of fresh water available at all times to pre-

CAUTION

If you feed your Sheltie a high-quality, nutritious dog food, it is unlikely that you need to add supplements. Adding supplements to a diet can disrupt the nutritional balance. An overdose of supplements is just as dangerous as a deficiency and can cause health problems. Consult your veterinarian before adding any supplements to your Sheltie's diet.

HOME BASICS
Dog Food Decisions

- Select a high-quality food that contains high-quality meat protein and fat.
- Animal-source protein is better for dogs because it provides the essential amino acids dogs need, in the correct balance. *Vegetarian diets are not recommended for dogs.*
- Choose a food with rice, wholesome grains, or potatoes for carbohydrate sources. Avoid foods that contain corn. Corn causes food allergies, itchy skin, and excessive weight gain in some dogs.
- Feed dry food whenever possible. Dry food is more filling and keeps teeth and gums healthier by helping to reduce plaque buildup. Canned food is more expensive and less nutritious by weight. Feed semi-moist foods sparingly, as they are high in sugar and low in quality.
- Be cautious of raw-food diets. Raw foods can contain dangerous bacteria such as *E. coli* and *Salmonella*, as well as bone particles that could cause choking or intestinal obstruction. Raw diets may not be nutritionally balanced.
- Limit treats to a reasonable amount and feed only healthful treats, such as dried "jerky" preservative-free chicken breast.

vent dehydration and illness. Your Sheltie loses body water throughout the day by panting, evaporation, footpad sweating, and in urine and feces. Water loss is greater in warm weather.

Your Sheltie will drink at least one ounce of water per pound of body weight per day, and much more if the weather is warm. Dogs that are active, pregnant, or lactating will also drink larger volumes of water. Sufficient water intake is especially important for older animals, because they often have reduced kidney (renal) function.

The best way to know if you are feeding your Sheltie the right food in the right amount is to look at him. If your Sheltie is healthy, alert, active, well muscled, and not over- or underweight, and has healthy skin and a beautiful coat—and he *enjoys* his food—then you are on the right track!

CAUTION

If your Sheltie is continually thirsty or drinks more than usual, it may be a warning sign for possible illness, such as diabetes or kidney disease.

If your Sheltie is not drinking enough, he can become dehydrated and develop health problems.

Consult your veterinarian if your Sheltie is drinking excessively or not drinking enough.

Chapter Seven

Training and Activities

When you chose a Sheltie to share your life, you didn't just choose the ultimate canine companion; you also chose the ultimate canine competitor! Shelties consistently win top honors at prestigious national events, ranking among the highest number of obedience and herding titled dogs of any breed. Shelties also have many high-level agility and tracking winners to their breed's credit. They are excellent farm dogs and guardians, wonderful therapy dogs, and skilled search-and-rescue dogs. Bright, enthusiastic, and eager to please, *Shelties are fun*! With the right training, a Sheltie can do just about anything—and do it very well.

When you brought your Sheltie home, you opened the door to the wonderful world of dog training and the innumerable activities you can do with your Sheltie. If you spend time with your Sheltie and train him well, he will make you proud of everything he does. If you decide to participate in various activities with your Sheltie, he will attract admirers like a magnet. In your shared adventures, you and your Sheltie will have a great time meeting like-minded Sheltie fans and making new friends.

Training

Today Shelties rank among the top 20 most popular breeds in the United States. This is not surprising. Devoted, beautiful, and brilliant, the Sheltie is the ultimate companion dog that loves to learn and wants to do things *with* his owner! Shelties are not independent dogs. They want to be with their people whenever possible, doing things *together*. Activities can range from a simple walk in the park to intense competitive events. Whatever activities you choose, your Sheltie will be eager to work and play with you. The fun activities that you can do together are limited only by your imagination.

Shelties learn quickly and are eager to please, but like all dogs, your Sheltie needs guidance to understand when he has done a good job or when he has erred. Your Sheltie will take his cues from you and do his best to please you. Shelties are sensitive to their owner's emotions and can also tell the difference between a happy face and a look of disapproval. A correction word, such as *no*, is usually sufficient to let a Sheltie know whether he has

Helpful Hints

To find a good puppy-training class, join a local dog club and ask other Sheltie owners which trainers they recommend. Your Sheltie's breeder and your veterinarian can also give you recommendations.

done well or not. Shelties respond very well to positive, kind training. *Harsh or forceful training techniques should never be used on a Sheltie.*

Shelties should never be punished for not performing an act perfectly, or for responding incorrectly to a command, or for not responding to a word or signal. When a dog first learns commands, he will make mistakes. It is up to the trainer to make sure there is no confusion and to teach and encourage the dog to follow the command correctly. Like everything else, it takes time, practice—and consistency.

When you train your Sheltie, be kind, consistent, and clear, and give lots of praise for a job well done. Also, remember that puppies have short attention spans, so a few short training sessions are better and more effective than one long training session. Always end a training session on a positive note and stop before your Sheltie is bored. Keep him eager to play the training game!

To be a good canine citizen and an acceptable member of society, in and outside the home, your Sheltie must learn some basic manners. For his safety, your Sheltie should learn the basic commands: *sit, down, stay, heel.*

FYI: Keys to Training Success

1. Be friendly, happy, encouraging, and enthusiastic so your Sheltie thinks training is a fun game.

2. Be patient, kind, and consistent in your training. When dogs make mistakes, it is often because of training or handling errors.

3. Make training corrections immediately. If you do not, your pet will not associate the correction with his mistake.

4. Keep training sessions short. End before your Sheltie is bored, and always end on a positive note.

5. Give a small food reward sometimes and lots of verbal praise always. Your pet needs continual reassurance that he is doing what you want him to do and is pleasing you!

How far beyond those commands you go depends on you and how much time you spend with your Sheltie. Your Sheltie is certainly capable of learning to do much more than the basics and would be delighted to learn new and different things!

Training a Shetland Sheepdog is a lot of fun! If you are bitten by the "training bug," you and your Sheltie may become competitive team members in one or more of the many dog sports, such as agility, obedience, herding, tracking, or fly ball. With a Sheltie, anything is possible.

Training starts the moment you bring your Sheltie home, and socialization is an integral part of training. The more people, places, and things your pet encounters in a positive way, the more outgoing and well adjusted he will be. A good way to start training and continue socialization is to enroll your Sheltie in a puppy-training class.

There are as many different training techniques as there are dogs and trainers. Before you sign up for a puppy class, ask for recommendations. Your puppy's breeder, your veterinarian, and other Sheltie owners will likely know some good trainers. Before you sign up for a puppy class, ask to visit a class while it is in session so you can decide if the trainer, your Sheltie, and you will make a good team. Shelties respond best to positive, fun training techniques. Shelties should never be subjected to harsh training techniques.

Helpful Hints

If you are comfortable when you train your Sheltie, training will be more enjoyable. Wear clothes that allow you to sit, stand, and kneel freely. Comfortable shoes help, too, especially if they have soft or rubber soles that won't hurt your Sheltie in case you accidentally step on his tiny toes. Set time aside for training when you are well rested, relaxed, and not in a hurry.

Basic Commands

Name

Your Sheltie has to learn his name so you can get his attention and communicate with him. Start by using his name when you play with him or feed him or want to get his attention. Whenever your puppy responds to his name, praise him profusely and sometimes give him a small food reward. It won't take your Sheltie long at all to know who he is.

CAUTION

Never call your Sheltie to you for the purposes of disciplining him if he misbehaves. He will not associate the reprimand with his misbehavior and will be confused. He will think you scolded him for coming to you when called. *Always* praise your Sheltie when he comes when called.

Come

Say your Sheltie's name to get his attention. Then say *"Come."* In the beginning, you can lure your pet with a small food reward to entice him to come to you, and then praise him when he does. You can also attach a 6 foot (1.8 m) leash to his collar so you can prevent him from leaving, if necessary, while you train him. Your Sheltie will quickly learn to come to you when called, purely for the attention you give him. Of course, you can still surprise him with a food reward now and then. Keeping him guessing is a good way to keep his attention and enthusiasm!

Sit

The *sit* command is the easiest of all commands to teach. Some people prefer to teach this command on a grooming table or tabletop so they do not have to kneel on the floor. If you prefer to teach on the ground, start by kneeling in front of your Sheltie. Hold a small piece of food over your Sheltie's nose, and raise your hand over his head. As his head goes up to follow the tidbit, his hindquarters will drop into a *sit* position. When this happens, say "*Yes*" or "*Good boy,*" or some other chosen phrase to use consistently to let your puppy know he has done the right thing. When you are ready to release your Sheltie from the *sit* command, you can say "Okay" or some other phrase to use consistently as a release word. With patience and consistency, your puppy will probably get the idea and learn to sit in just a few training sessions. As you practice more, you can gradually extend the duration of the *sit*.

Down

You can teach this command on the tabletop or on the floor. If you work on the floor, start by kneeling with your Sheltie on your left side and ask him to sit. Praise him when he sits. Next, show him you have a food reward and lower it to the floor and say *"Down."* His nose will follow the treat, and if you are lucky, he may lie down to eat the treat. Usually, however, you have to first show him what is expected of him. Gently grasp his forelegs in your right hand and pull his forelegs forward so that he must lie

down. When he is in the *down* position, say "Yes!" and give him a small food reward. In the beginning, you may also have to place your hand on his shoulders to remind him to remain lying down until you give him the release word, such as *"Okay."* This command will take some time to master. As your Sheltie learns this command, you may also use a palm-down, downward motion of your hand to signal the *down* command. As with other commands, you will eventually replace the food reward with praise alone.

Stay

After your Sheltie has learned the *come, sit,* and *down* commands, you can work on *sit-stay* and *down-stay*. *Stay* is a very important command and can come in handy in emergency situations. It is also a tough command because your Sheltie wants to be *with* you. Up to now you have been training him to come to you and do things. Now, you are asking him to remain in place while you walk *away* from him! It's not surprising that this can be confusing for your pet in the beginning.

Although some people prefer to teach Shelties the *sit* and *down* commands on a tabletop, it is not safe to teach the *stay* command on a tabletop because your Sheltie may jump from the tabletop and injure himself. Also, you need to be able to step on the leash in case your pet starts to leave, so the *stay* command is taught on the ground.

Some trainers prefer to teach the *stay* command first in the sitting position: the *sit-stay*. Others prefer to first teach the *stay* command in the down position: the *down-stay*.

It is important to get your Sheltie's attention and make eye contact. Put the palm of your right hand in front of his face and say *"Stay."* Wait a few seconds, maintaining eye contact. If your Sheltie remains in position, say "Good stay" and give him a treat. If he gets up to leave, step on the leash to prevent him from leaving, make him sit, and start over.

At first, you will be only a few feet away from him, but over time you will be able to take a few steps back, or to the side, or turn your back to him. Always come back to your Sheltie to reward him with a food treat so he realizes that *you* come to *him* with treats and that, in this situation, he does not come to you for rewards. Use a special release phrase, such as "Free" or "All done" to let him know when he no longer has to *stay*.

Little by little, with each training session, you will be able to increase the time he remains in position and the distance you are away from him. As you train your Sheltie, *extend the time first, then the distance*. You will eventually give the treat only before you signal he has been released from the *stay* command.

Wait

After your Sheltie learns to stay, *wait* will be an easy command for him to learn. *Wait* is similar to *stay*, but different in that it is a brief holding time and often involves waiting by your side, or near you, and often at doorways and thresholds. Your Sheltie can wait in a sitting, standing, or lying position.

Wait is a very valuable training command, because it keeps your pet safe. It teaches him to wait for you while you are near his side but may be busy doing something else and not focusing on him. For example, you might be trying to untangle a leash or attach a collar, or you might be checking traffic to see if it is safe to let your pet out of the car. You might be trying to shift the leash to a free hand so you can pick up par-

Breed Truths

1. Shelties are perfectionists. They are able to concentrate and focus on the job and do their work with precision.
2. Shelties are enthusiastic when they work and play. They enjoy what they do.
3. Shelties take subtle cues from their handlers and respond to positive reward training. Shelties are easy to handle and very responsive to their trainers.
4. Shelties should *never* be subjected to force or to harsh training techniques.

cels or luggage. *Wait* teaches your Sheltie to remain in place and gives you control of your pet. For example, if you are opening the front door, you can tell your Sheltie to *wait* so he doesn't rush past you, into the neighbor's yard, or out into the street. If you are getting your pet out of his travel crate, you can tell him to *wait* so you can first put his collar on him and attach his leash and he doesn't jump out of the car, injure himself, or run into trouble.

The *wait* command should first be taught indoors. You can use a door threshold, such as one between a bedroom and a hall, and place your Sheltie on one side of the threshold with you standing on the other side. Place your palm in front of your pet's face and say *"Wait."* If he tries to cross the threshold, put him back in place and say *"Wait."* When you are ready for him to cross the threshold, say *"Okay,"* or use some other release word to tell him he can cross the doorway, and praise him. You can later practice closing the door, opening it and telling your Sheltie to wait, and then telling him when it is all right to cross the doorway.

Leash Training

Studies have shown that leash training is easiest when introduced to a puppy between the ages of five and nine weeks. Leash training actually begins without a leash. It begins with teaching your puppy to come when called and then to follow you around the house or yard. Once these simple goals are accomplished, your Sheltie puppy can wear a light safety collar (such as a break-away collar), but only when he is being directly supervised by you. Next, attach a light line, such as yarn or a string, and let your puppy drag it around. When he is used to this, you can attach a very light leash, such as a thin show lead. Do not tug or pull on the lead. If your puppy protests or pulls against the leash, do not scold or drag him. Talk to him and lure him to you and reward him. Then encourage your puppy to follow you. Lure him with a small treat, if necessary. He will learn that he is being

FYI: Top of the Class

Dog-training classes are a lot of fun and very rewarding. By participating in training classes, your Sheltie will become a model canine citizen, a wonderful ambassador for the breed, and a keen competitor—and you will form many lasting friendships.

As your Sheltie graduates from each training level, you may well find him at the top of his class. Your Sheltie may be an excellent candidate for herding, or for obedience and agility, or for any of the many other canine competitive sports. Suddenly you realize that all that basic training is just the beginning. When it comes to dog activities and events, there is no finish line!

rewarded for walking with you. Keep him to your left side and start with short distances, such as across the living room. Later extend the distance to across the backyard. Your Sheltie may weave a bit, or run a little ahead, or drop behind, but you can continue to encourage him to keep alongside of you. As long as your puppy walks with you, reward him with praise and a treat. Make it a game!

Heel

After your Sheltie has learned to follow you and walk with you, you can teach him to *heel*. At this point, a slip collar or a very fine choke chain (such as those used in dog shows) can be used. It is important to remove the collar whenever you are not directly supervising your dog. Lure your

CAUTION

To prevent accidental choking or strangulation, never leave your Sheltie puppy alone when he is wearing a collar or leash, and never tie your Sheltie to any objects.

Sheltie to your left side, ask him to sit, and attach a light leash to his collar. Introduce the word *heel* and start walking. When your Sheltie walks alongside of you and keeps up with you, praise him. If he pulls on the leash, stop and make him come back to your side. Say "*Heel*" and begin walking again, and as he comes along, reward him with a treat. This teaches him that he is rewarded only when he is at your left side. When you stop walking, tell your Sheltie to sit and make sure he sits at your left side. When you are ready to start walking again, say "*Heel*."

As your Sheltie improves at heeling, you can vary your speed and praise him as long as he keeps pace with you without pulling on the leash. The leash should not be pulled taut. When your Sheltie is heeling correctly, the leash will be slack, not tight.

Soon, you and your Sheltie will be going on leisurely strolls, enjoying every step of the way!

Activities

Herding

The herding instinct is a dog's desire to try to control the movement of livestock. Shelties were originally selected, bred, and raised for their abilities as robust working farm dogs with herding instinct, eagerness to do the farmer's bidding, and skill at gathering livestock. Selection was based primarily on working and herding ability, and less on appearance. Later, more emphasis was placed on selecting Shelties for their beauty and for the show ring. Many breeders became concerned that Shelties might lose their natural herding instinct and working ability. The American Shetland Sheepdog Association conducted herding tests on Shelties and confirmed that many Shelties still retain their natural instincts. Sheltie breeders strive to produce Shetland Sheepdogs of exquisite beauty that conform to the breed standard and retain their natural herding and working instincts and true Sheltie characteristics and temperament.

Every dog is different, and some Shelties have more herding instinct than others. Some Shelties do not show their instinct until they are adolescents or young adults.

Shelties want to control objects in motion and work by gathering. Shelties that are not working on farms may show herding instinct in a variety of ways, such as chasing a bicycle or trying to round up children in a yard. The best way to know how keen your Sheltie's herding instinct is, however, is to

FYI: The Herding Instinct Program

In 1986, the American Shetland Sheepdog Association (ASSA) began the herding instinct program. Of approximately 1,000 Shelties demonstrating herding instinct, the ASSA noted a variety of working tendencies among them. The ASSA reported the following findings:

84% of the Shelties demonstrated a "gathering style" of working and moved around the handler and the livestock.

9% of the Shelties showed no clear working style.

32% tended to move wide around the stock on approach, and 68% tended to move close.

25% of the Shelties barked significantly while working.

40% of the Shelties barked only in situations where the stock showed some resistance.

35% of the Shelties were quiet workers.

2% of the dogs demonstrated a "strong eye," that is, they had an intent gaze toward the stock, with pausing approach and lowered body stance.

40% showed "medium eye," an intent concentration, but a freer, upright manner of moving.

58% showed "loose eye," meaning the dog has good concentration on the stock, but is free-moving and takes in a wider view of the overall scene.

Shelties tend to predominantly fetch or gather, and those with true natural driving style are rare.

test him with livestock. Herding instinct can be tested using ducks or sheep. Dog clubs routinely offer herding instinct testing and certification for anyone who wants to test their dog's herding instinct and natural ability.

If your Sheltie demonstrates herding instinct and you want to become involved in the sport, you have many options. In 1990, the American Kennel Club (AKC) began two levels of noncompetitive tests, three trial levels, and a herding championship. With each level the course, obstacles, and challenges become more difficult as your dog advances. There is a lot to learn about herding! You can obtain detailed information about these programs from the AKC (see Resources) and the American Herding Breeds Association (AHBA).

- Test levels: Herding Tested (HT) and Pre-Trial (PT)
- Trial classes: Herding Started (HS) A course, Herding Intermediate (HI) B course, and Herding Excellent (HX) C course
- Herding Championship

In addition, the American Herding Breeds Association offers a series of trials and tests:

- Herding Capability Tested (HCT)
- Junior Herding (JHD)
- Herding Dog Trial I, II, and III (HDT-I, HDT-II, HDT-III)
- Herding Trial Champion (HTCH)

Agility

Agility is the American Kennel Club's most popular competitive sport. It is an exciting, challenging, fast-paced, timed event that is as much fun for the spectators as it is for the competitors. Dogs complete challenging obstacle courses, jump over objects, teeter on seesaws, run on planks, dive through tunnels, leap through hoops, and weave between poles.

Titles that can be earned, in increasing level of difficulty, are Novice Agility (NA), Open Agility (OA), Agility Excellent (AX), and Master Agility Excellent (MX).

Agility tests a dog's versatility, athleticism, and ability to work together with its handler. It's no wonder that Shelties are always top winners in this event! In fact, Shelties consistently make up 20 percent or more of the American Kennel Club's top 20 agility dogs listed every year.

3 When he walks alongside of you, give him a treat and ask him to "*Heel*". Continue to give him a treat and praise him as he learns to keep pace with you. If he pulls on the leash, stop and make him come back to your side. Say "*Heel*" and begin walking again and as he comes along, give him a treat. This teaches him that he is only rewarded when he is at your side and that there is no reward if he is a distance away from you.

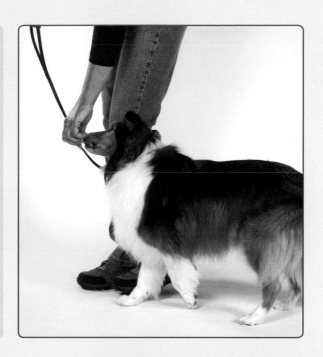

4 After he has learned *heel* at a walk, you can increase the speed to a fast walk or a jog. Give him a treat and praise him often as he keeps pace with you and walks alongside of you without pulling on the leash. When he performs *heel* well on the leash, you can practice the command in a safe, enclosed area with him off leash.

The Sit Command

1 Call your Sheltie to you. Kneel in front of him and show him that you have a treat. Raise your hand holding the treat above his head. If he jumps and tries to get the treat, close your hand around it. Make eye contact and hold his attention.

2 Raise your hand holding the treat just above his head. As his nose follows your hand up, he must lower his rump. The moment his rump touches the ground and he is in a sitting position, say "Yes!" and quickly reward him with the treat. Give him lots of praise.

3 When he has learned this action, use the word *"Sit."* In the beginning, he will not understand that he is to remain sitting until you give a release signal, such as *"Good boy"* or *"Okay."* If he tries to get up and leave before you give the release signal, get his attention again by showing him a treat and raising it above his head, making him *sit* again.

4 After he has learned the meaning of the command *sit*, you can extend the time gradually so that he remains sitting for a longer period of time. You can also use the hand signal at the same time you give the command, so that he learns that the word and the hand signal are both a command to *sit*.

The Stay Command

1 Say your Sheltie's name to get his attention. Call him to you and attach his leash. Show him that you have a treat. Give him the command to *sit*. Praise him.

2 Make eye contact. Put the palm of your right hand in front of his face and say "*Stay*." Wait a few seconds, maintaining eye contact. When he remains in position, calmly say "*Good stay*" and give him a treat. If he tends to get up to try to leave, step on the leash to prevent him from leaving. Get his attention, say "*Sit*" and start over.

3 When he stays in place, take another step backward, wait a few seconds, then lean forward and give him another treat and praise him. Say, "*Good stay*." Next, partially turn away from him, wait a slightly longer period of time, then turn back facing him. Return to him, give him a treat and say, "*Good stay*." This way he learns that he does not come to you for rewards. You go to him and he stays in place.

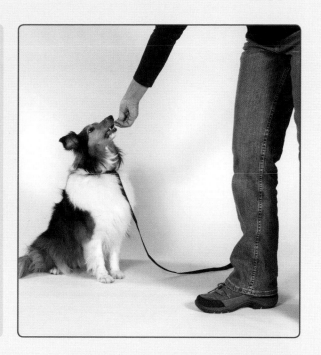

4 As he stays in place, continue to reward him periodically with treats. Take a few additional steps back, or step to the side, or turn your back. Gradually extend the time between treats and praise. Use a release signal, such as "*All done!*" to let him know when the training session is over.

Chapter Eight

Grooming

Grooming is an essential part of your Shetland Sheepdog's health-care program. One of the most appealing features that sets your Sheltie apart from most other breeds— and surely a big reason why you were attracted to your dog from the very beginning—is his beautiful, glamorous coat. Shelties are widely recognized and admired for their stunning coats and lovely colors. It is not surprising that they consistently win top awards in conformation events worldwide—just as your Sheltie has won your heart. But a gorgeous coat is not created overnight, and not every Sheltie can grow and maintain a fabulous, sensational coat. A beautiful coat is the result of excellent health care, high-quality nutrition, and the right combination of genes (inheritance).

Shelties have a double coat. The outer coat is harsh, straight, and long. The undercoat is short, furry, and dense and adds to the coat's "standoff" appearance. Surprisingly, despite the thick undercoat and large amount and length of hair, a healthy Sheltie's coat requires very little in the way of equipment or products to keep it looking great. The key is to brush the coat thoroughly, from the skin out, at least once a week. This keeps the skin healthy and maintains the coat in top condition, free of mats and tangles. Of course, if your Sheltie goes outside and runs through fields and accumulates weeds, seeds, stickers, parasites, dirt, and debris in his coat, then his coat will need a thorough brushing that same day. The longer you wait, the more difficult your pet's coat will be to groom, and mats will form. Mats cause the coat to lose its insulating ability and also make ideal hiding places for parasites. Mats create a moist environment where bacteria can multiply and where skin sores and "hot spots" can quickly develop.

When your Sheltie is shedding large quantities of hair, especially the undercoat, he may need daily brushing until the coat has shed out completely (breeders call this "blowing coat") and the new coat has started to replace it. During heaving shedding, the undercoat can come out in large, cottony clumps. This is normal.

Shelties *love* to be groomed. They thrive on the personal attention they receive from their owners during grooming sessions, and they surely feel much better after a stimulating, refreshing brushing. Grooming is good for your Sheltie, and it can be good for you, too. It can be a fun form of relaxation. It has been well documented that touching and caressing a dog can help lower blood pressure. Studies have also shown that when people touch

FYI: Growing a Show Coat

A beautiful show coat starts when you purchase your Sheltie from a reputable breeder. Coat quality, density, length, texture, and color are inherited from the parents. If your Sheltie did not inherit the genes that produce a stunning show coat, then all the products in the world (shampoos, rinses, nutritional supplements, brushes, and combs) won't produce a champion show coat. This doesn't mean that your Sheltie won't benefit from special hair care and products to help him look and feel his very best. He will! It simply means you must be realistic in your expectations.

their dogs, oxytocin (a hormone that plays an important role in bonding, trust, stress reduction, and a desire for social connection) is released in both the owner *and* the dog. Grooming strengthens the friendship bond between you and your Sheltie!

Grooming Supplies

You do not need much equipment to keep your Sheltland Sheepdog looking and feeling his best, but the equipment you use should be good quality.

CHECKLIST

Grooming Supplies

- ✔ Grooming table with nonslip mat
- ✔ Brush with flexible pins and without balls on the tips of the pins
- ✔ Slicker brush (for thicker parts of coat)
- ✔ Bristle brush
- ✔ Steel comb with rounded teeth, half-medium spacing, teeth 1 inch (2.5 cm) long
- ✔ Stripping stone
- ✔ Flea comb
- ✔ Scissors, stainless steel, blunt-tipped, straight
- ✔ Shears, stainless steel, curved, 7 inches (18 cm)
- ✔ Shears, stainless steel, straight, 7 inches (18 cm)
- ✔ Eye ointment to protect eyes during bath
- ✔ Nail trimmers, guillotine-type
- ✔ Nail grinder
- ✔ Styptic powder
- ✔ Spray bottle
- ✔ De-tangling spray
- ✔ Emollient shampoo (pH balanced for dog skin)
- ✔ Hair rinse developed for dogs
- ✔ Ear-cleaning solution (available from your veterinarian)
- ✔ Cotton-tipped swabs
- ✔ Cotton balls
- ✔ Washcloth
- ✔ Paper towels
- ✔ Hair dryer
- ✔ Toothbrush
- ✔ Toothpaste developed for dogs
- ✔ Small portable vacuum for cleanup
- ✔ Plastic bags to discard hair

Whenever possible, invest in the best tools you can. Good equipment will give better results, last longer, and make grooming a lot easier.

Your Sheltie's Coat

Hair Growth

The important relationship between hair growth and high-quality nutrition cannot be overemphasized. Hair is made up of almost solid protein, called keratin. A balanced diet containing high-quality, digestible protein is essential for your Sheltie to grow a beautiful coat.

Fun Facts

Male Shelties have a bigger, fuller coat than female Shelties.

Your Sheltie's hair grows in cycles. The active growth cycle is called the anagen phase. The catagen phase is a transitional period leading to the resting phase. The telogen phase is when hair is retained in the hair follicle as "dead hair." This dead hair is eventually shed. Dogs typically shed in a mosaic pattern throughout the body. Brushing removes dead hairs, stimulates the skin, and distributes natural oils in the coat.

During the anagen phase, a single hair grows only .1 to .2 mm each day. However, if you multiply that distance times the hundreds of thousands of growing hairs on your Sheltie's body, that totals more than 50 feet (15 m) of hair growth each day! A Sheltie in poor health or receiving an inadequate diet can have delayed or arrested hair growth, a dull coat, and weak hair that breaks easily.

Shedding

Depending on geographical location, photoperiod, weather, and seasons, most Shelties tend to do their major shedding during the summer. The new coat grows in during the early fall and attains full glory during the winter months. This makes sense, because a heavy coat would be needed most in winter. However, not all Shelties fit a specific pattern for coat growth and hair loss. For example, after a female gives birth to a litter, she normally sheds her coat six to eight weeks later. This hair loss is called post-partum effluvium and is entirely normal.

A Sheltie with the genetic potential to grow a gorgeous coat will not be able to do so unless it is in excellent health, receives the best of care and nutritious food, and the environmental conditions are just right. When a Sheltie is sick, stressed, fed an inadequate diet, or has some hormonal imbalances, the coat may shed excessively and not grow. Many skin and hair problems are caused by poor nutrition, food allergies, parasites (internal and external), fungi, harsh chemicals or inappropriate products used on the skin, allergies to synthetic bedding material, or an unsanitary damp environment. Shelties can also develop dry, flaky skin during the winter when they are exposed to the drying effects of heaters, radiators, and fireplaces.

Training Your Sheltie to Be Groomed

Sheltie owners develop their own individual grooming methods that work best for them and give them the desired results for their particular dogs. You can learn more tips on how to groom your Sheltie by talking with other Sheltie owners, Shelties breeders, groomers, and show handlers.

Some people like to groom their dogs while sitting on the floor, but most people find it more convenient to sit on a chair and groom their pet while it is on a grooming table. Working on a table top makes it possible to work in various positions at a comfortable level, without bending or stooping.

Table Training

You can start training your Sheltie to be groomed on a table when he is a puppy, *after* he has learned the commands *sit* and *down*. Later, when he has had more training, he can also learn to stand on the table.

Begin by having your Sheltie lie on his side on the table. Praise him as you gently brush him with a soft brush. If you need him to stand while you brush him, hold him with your hand lightly between the rear legs so if he

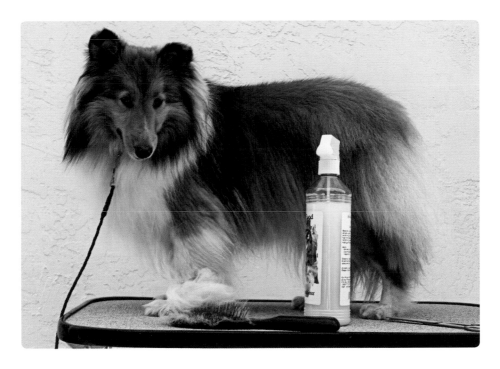

tries to move or sit down, you can bring him back to a standing position. Handle his head, ears, feet, and mouth. Your puppy must become used to this handling so you can check his eyes, clean his ears, trim his toenails, and brush his teeth routinely.

In a short time, you can introduce your puppy to the spray bottle so he can get used to the sound it makes. When he is used to the spray bottle, you can use it to lightly dampen his coat when you brush it, as necessary.

Every time you groom your Sheltie, check his eyes to make sure they are clear. Using a soft, clean, damp cloth, gently clean around the eyes and remove any discharge or dirt that has accumulated in the inner corners. Check that the lid margins are not swollen and that there is no material dried in the eyelashes. Use a clean, soft, damp, cloth to clean the corners of the nostrils where dirt may accumulate. Dampen a cotton ball with a gentle ear cleaner. Ear solutions containing alcohol or other irritating substances that burn should be avoided. Clean the inside of the ears carefully. Do not allow liquid to run down into the ear canal. Do not push cotton swabs down your pet's ear canals.

Make the first grooming training sessions short, just a few minutes. Extend the time period a little longer each session. Always end on a happy note and praise your puppy. Give him a treat for good behavior. It won't be long before your Sheltie learns the routine and is eager for you to lift him onto the table to be brushed again!

Never leave your puppy unsupervised on the grooming table! He could fall off and injure himself.

Brushing and Trimming

Head

Check your Sheltie's eyes, ears, nose, and mouth. Clean the ears gently, if needed. Brush the hair on the side of the face. You can also smooth the hair on the sides of the face with a stripping stone.

Gently comb the hair on and around the ears with a fine-toothed comb, such as a flea comb. With blunt-tipped scissors, trim straggling hairs on the back of the ear and around the ear tip. Check the fine hairs on the outer sides of the base of the ears. These hairs are more prone to tangle and form small knots. If they are not kept combed out regularly, they can form mats. If your Sheltie's hair is tangled, use a gentle de-tangling solution or spray developed for dogs. Wet the hair, and then gently comb out the tangles.

Trim away excess hair in front of the ear, so that it does not extend more than halfway up the inside of the ear.

Line Brushing

Line brushing is a basic method that lets you groom your Sheltie's hair through to the skin, in sections, layer by layer. Start at the back of the head and top of the neck and separate your pet's hair in a line, down to the skin. Brush the coat well, then move down the neck, divide off another section of hair, and brush through that. Continue in this manner until you have groomed down the neck and down the side of the body, brushed the hip and thigh, and ended at the croup.

Many groomers prefer to brush the hair on the neck and body against the direction of hair growth, a technique called backbrushing, when they line-brush. Others brush first in the direction of hair growth, removing as much dead hair as possible, and then backbrush. The technique you choose to groom your Sheltie will depend on the amount of coat he has and its condition.

Spraying the coat lightly with water as you line-brush can help make it easier for the brush to glide. There are also light spray "leave-in" conditioners and de-tangling solutions available that can be used for this purpose.

Helpful Hints

Puppy Ears

Sheltie ears are supposed to naturally tip over at the top. Naturally tipping ears is an inherited trait. When Shelties are very young puppies, their ears may tip, but about the time their teeth are coming in, some puppies' ears may start to stand up straight, giving them a foxy appearance. This is called "prick" or "erect" ears. Breeders often tape, brace, or weight a Sheltie puppy's ears to train the ears to tip if they do not tip naturally. There are many different "ear training" techniques, some more successful than others. If your Sheltie's ears start to rise and you do not want them to remain erect, contact the breeder for advice.

The back of the thigh has dense, long hair (called the "pants" or "skirts"). This hair should be brushed out carefully to separate all of the hair without injuring the delicate skin on the back of the thighs.

Brush out the tail completely, working from the base of the tail and separating the hairs all the way to the tip of the tail.

Brush the front legs, paying special attention to the axillary (armpit) area, where hair tends to tangle and mat. Brush out the long hair on the back of the front legs, all the way down the pasterns to the feet. Brush out the hair on the rear legs from the hock down. A flea comb is handy to remove fine, dead hair on the hocks and pasterns.

When a Sheltie has not been groomed regularly, knots and mats can form at the base of the ears, in the axillary area, in the groin or inner thigh, and around the base of the scrotum. Hair may also tend to mat under the tail, near the anus or vulva. Tangles or mats in these delicate areas should be removed gently and very carefully with a hair de-tangling product. If mats are too thick to remove with a brush or comb, the mats can be cut or gently teased out with blunt-tipped scissors, taking great care not to accidentally cut the skin.

Trim the legs and feet after the toenails are trimmed.

Helpful Hints

If your Sheltie's coat needs a lot of grooming, you may choose to split grooming into two or three sessions so you and your Sheltie don't become too tired or bored with the project. Grooming should be fun for both of you. Stop grooming while your Sheltie is still happy and enjoying all of the attention you are lavishing on him so you can end the session on a positive note!

BE PREPARED! Trimming Toenails

Shelties need to have their toenails trimmed regularly. Overgrown nails can interfere with movement and hinder your Sheltie's movement and walking ability.

There are a variety of types of nail trimmers. Guillotine-style clippers work well for Shelties. To use these, place the toenail inside the metal loop, align the upper and lower blades with the area to cut, and squeeze the clipper handles.

To determine if your Sheltie's nails need to be trimmed, stand him on the grooming table and examine them. None of the nails should touch the surface of the table. Notice that each toenail curves and tapers into a point. If the toenail is light, you will see the pink interior, or the "quick." This is the blood supply. Just below the quick is the curved tip of the nail that needs to be removed. If the nails are dark, illumination with a penlight to find the quick may be helpful. If the toenails are too dark to differentiate where the quick ends, cut the tip of the nail where it begins to curve. Cut only the very tip of the toenail. If you cut too close, stop the bleeding by applying styptic powder (a clotting powder that is available from pet stores) or a styptic stick (human shaving sticks).

A nail grinder can be used to trim nails and smooth the tips. *Use caution so that you do not overheat the nails while using the nail grinder.*

Trim your Sheltie's toenails before you trim his feet.

Feet

Use blunt-tipped scissors to trim around the feet and footpads. Comb the hair between the toes and on the top of the foot up, and then trim. This technique makes the foot look naturally neat and trim without giving it a straight, severe, sharp-cut look.

Helpful Hints

Dewclaws (vestigial digits located where a "thumb" would be) are usually removed at three days of age, but if your Sheltie has dewclaws, trim them. Untrimmed dewclaws can snag and tear, or grow into footpads and tissues, causing pain and lameness.

Excessive hair between the toes causes the foot to splay. Keeping the feet neatly trimmed prevents mats, dirt, foreign objects (such as grass awns and stickers), and excess moisture (leading to bacterial growth and sores) from accumulating between the toes.

Pasterns and Hocks

There are different ways to trim the pasterns and hocks. Some of the techniques vary according to what is currently fashionable in the show ring.

Pasterns: Pull the front leg forward so you can see the back of the footpad.

Comb the hairs on the pastern straight out, perpendicular to the ground. Starting at the back of the footpad, using a large pair of scissors or shears, trim the loose hairs all the way up to the small pad on the back of the forelimb. Do not trim the "feathering" above the pad!

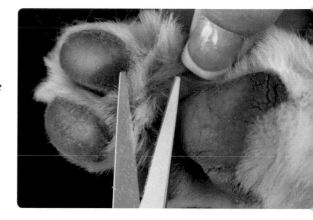

Hocks: Stand your Sheltie on the grooming table and comb the hair on the hocks straight out, perpendicular to the ground. Starting slightly below the hock joint, trim away uneven and stray hairs in a straight, vertical line using long, curved shears. Curved shears are better to use than regular scissors, because they make the trimmed area look natural, rather than having a sharp, harsh appearance. Next, comb the hair on the hock to the inside of the leg, and again trim in a vertical line, removing uneven hairs. Finally, comb the hair on the hock to the outside of the leg and trim away remaining stray hairs in a vertical line. The hair on the hock should now have a smooth, rounded, tidy, and natural appearance.

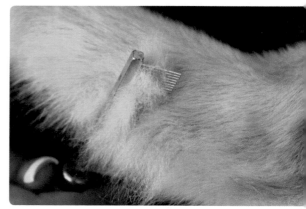

Bathing

Shelties are naturally very clean. Your Sheltie does not have to be bathed frequently, but he should have a bath when he needs one. How often you bathe your Sheltie will depend on his activities and environment. There are many gentle shampoos on the market, especially emollient (nonsoap) shampoos that are gentle on the skin and coat and rinse out easily. Use products developed for dogs, not for humans, as dog shampoos are pH balanced for dog skin. Some dog shampoos are developed for specific coat colors, such as black, white, and blue (gray).

Groom your Sheltie before you bathe him. Fill the tub with a few inches of lukewarm water. Put cotton in your Sheltie's ears so water doesn't get into the ear canals, and put him in the tub. With a sprayer, soak his coat with lukewarm water until it is saturated. Starting at the top of the back of the neck, add shampoo and massage it through the coat, working down the back to the rump. Shampoo the sides of the body, the belly, the limbs, and under the tail. Suds and rub the feet, and shampoo the tail. Gently wash the head and ears, being careful not to let soap get in your Sheltie's eyes and

Helpful Hints

Brush your Sheltie *before* you give him a bath. If you don't remove loose hair, knots, tangles, and mats before you bathe your pet, they will become fixed in the coat when it gets wet and will be even more difficult to remove.

keeping water from entering the ears. Alternatively, you can wipe the top of the head, sides of the face, and muzzle with a clean, damp cloth.

When you are finished shampooing your Sheltie, use the sprayer to rinse the coat thoroughly with lukewarm water. Adding a moisturizing rinse to the coat will help keep it clean and easier to brush. Some kinds of moisturizers can be left in, others must be rinsed out before drying.

Blot your Sheltie with a towel to remove most of the water, and then dry him with a hair dryer (a forced-air hair dryer speeds up the job). Make sure the hair dryer setting is not too hot, and don't hold the hair dryer too close to the skin, so you don't burn your pet. While drying the coat you can closely inspect the skin as the dryer separates the hairs. When your Sheltie is almost dry, you can brush him while you finish drying him.

Dental Care

Dental care is one of the most important aspects of your Sheltie's health-care program. Start training your Sheltie for dental care when he is a puppy.

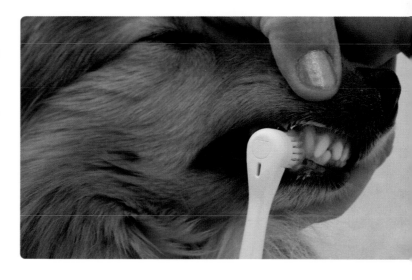

Sheltie puppies are born without teeth. When they reach three to four weeks of age, their deciduous teeth (baby teeth) start to erupt. Within a few months the 28 temporary teeth start to fall out and are replaced by 48 permanent teeth. By six months of age, the adult teeth have erupted. These teeth must last your dog's lifetime, so it is important to take good care of them by preventing plaque and tartar buildup and periodontal disease.

The best way to reduce plaque buildup is by dental brushing. You can train your Sheltie to dental brushing by practicing on his deciduous teeth while he is a puppy. In the beginning, keep dental brushing sessions short so your puppy will tolerate them better. Praise him for good behavior. By the time he is an adult, he will be used to the routine.

Breed Truths

Bad breath in Shelties is a possible sign of health problems:

- periodontal disease
- foreign body obstructing nasal passages (such as a grass awn or nasal tumor)
- infection or ulcers
- metabolic diseases

Use a soft bristle brush and a toothpaste designed specifically for dogs. Start with the upper front teeth (incisors), brushing down and away from the gum line, or in a gentle, circular motion. Proceed back to the premolars and molars on each side of the mouth. Repeat the same procedure for the bottom teeth.

The loving care you give your Sheltie is reflected in his beautiful coat and overall condition. Your Sheltie will feel great in his clean, well-groomed, and glorious coat, and he will love the attention he receives from you when you groom him. He will also receive a lot of attention when you take him out on walks. Your beautiful companion will attract admirers like a magnet. Your Sheltie doesn't have to be formally competing in the show ring to look fantastic. He knows that he is always "Best in Show" in your eyes—and that's all that matters to him!

Chapter Nine

The Senior Shetland Sheepdog

People often lose their hearts to puppies, but a senior Sheltie can charm the soul like no other dog can. Your love and appreciation for your Sheltie will grow with every passing year. His companionship and friendship will be ever more precious to you the longer you are together. And there's more good news. Shelties live longer than most breeds, with an average life span of 13 to 15 years. Many Shelties live even longer. With excellent care and nutrition, that puppy you fell in love with that has joined your family may live well into his teens!

When people plan to add a dog to their families, they usually think of acquiring a puppy. It seems obvious, but is worth reminding ourselves that a dog is a puppy for only a very short time. By 18 months of age, a Sheltie has started the young-adult phase of his life. The mature-adult stage is from two to seven years of age. Then, at age seven, dogs are considered to be "seniors."

The term *senior* is a generalization that takes all dog breeds into consideration, but there are breed variations and individual variations that determine how a dog changes with age and how rapidly these aging changes occur. For example, smaller breeds usually live longer than large or giant breeds. A seven-year-old Sheltie may be just halfway through his life and show only mild signs of aging. In contrast, a seven-year-old Great Dane may have only three years left to live and show significant signs of aging. Both dogs may be "seniors," but health-wise they are not the same. Another way of looking at it is that Shelties are "middle-aged" when they reach seven years of age, compared with many breeds that do not have the longevity that Shelties enjoy.

Like humans, some Shelties age more slowly and have fewer health problems than others. Just because your Sheltie turned seven years old doesn't mean he will suddenly start to deteriorate and that the next several years will be filled with health problems. Shelties that receive excellent care and nutrition throughout their lives tend to remain more "youthful" for their age when compared with many other breeds. Often, the first signs of aging are so subtle in a Sheltie that they go unnoticed by the owner and are detected by the veterinarian during a routine health checkup.

FYI: Signs of Aging

Signs of Aging	Problems
Gray, white, or silver hairs, especially along the sides of the face, eyebrows, muzzle	None
Less-supple skin, body odor, thin coat, warts, moles, cysts, lumps, and growths on skin	Odor may indicate health problem, growths may be cancerous
Tires easily and takes longer, more frequent naps; changes in sleep patterns	Aging heart or heart failure, or other organ problems
Arthritis and muscle disuse atrophy	Joint pain or trauma, muscle weakness, lack of muscle mass; stiff or painful movement, difficulty rising, sitting, or lying down; weak or wobbly in the hindquarters
Slow metabolic rate	Metabolism slows with aging, leading to weight gain and obesity in some Shelties. Obesity can lead to joint pain, diabetes, heart disease, other health problems.
Bad breath, difficulty eating, plaque and tartar accumulation on teeth, swollen gums, periodontal disease, oral tumors, nasal tumors	Dental disease can lead to infections, bacteria in the bloodstream, and abscesses in the heart, liver, kidney, and other organs.
Failing eyesight, cataracts	Some cataracts are caused by aging, some are caused by diabetes.
Impaired hearing, deafness	As hearing fails and eyesight worsens, Shelties rely more on their sense of smell.
Urinary incontinence or increased urination	Ranging from dribbling to complete lack of control—the condition is more common in geriatric, spayed females than in males. Excessive urination can be caused by kidney or liver disease, diabetes, Cushing's syndrome, infection.
Bowel problems	Diarrhea and constipation or lack of bowel control may be caused by food intolerance, malabsorption, diseases (such as kidney disease), neurological problems, and tumors of the gastrointestinal tract.
Breathing difficulties, coughing	Heart disease, lung cancer, infection, other
Decreased immunity and lowered disease resistance	Deterioration of the immune system, immune suppression, auto-immune diseases, stress
Senility, disorientation, cognitive dysfunction	Multiple causes, including normal aging, toxicity caused by organ failure, brain cell destruction, and brain tumor. May forget to eliminate in appropriate places and is confused.
Overall health deterioration, lack of appetite, weight loss	Multiple causes, including heart, liver, kidney, pancreas, lungs, and other organ disease or failure; cancer; hormonal imbalances; stress

What You Can Do

Nothing

Provide good nutrition, groom regularly for skin and coat care, bathe when needed, using a gentle shampoo and rinse, have your veterinarian check any observed growths

Prescription medications are available, if needed. Rest, prevent stress, avoid excessive exercise.

Prevent jumping; avoid stairs, hills, hard surfaces, and excessive or strenuous exercise. Consult your veterinarian for exam, x rays, and medicine for pain and inflammation.

Feed correct diet for age and activity level, do not overfeed, weigh your Sheltie weekly.

Dental cleaning, tooth extractions, surgery, and antibiotics—consult your veterinarian.

Speak to your Sheltie as you approach him, so you do not startle him. Extend your hand so he can smell you. Do not change his environment or relocate furniture in the home.

Use hand signals to communicate and approach him so he can see you. Extend your hand so he can detect your scent.

Consult your veterinarian for a diagnosis and to rule out serious kidney, bladder, or neurological problems. Medications are available to help treat the condition.

A special or prescription diet may be helpful. Consult your veterinarian.

Consult your veterinarian

Give your Sheltie special attention, such as a gentle brushing or a massage. Consult your veterinarian.

Prescription medicine is available to treat dogs with cognitive dysfunction. Stimulate your Sheltie's cognitive function by spending lots of time interacting with him. Refresh his memory by asking him to do something, such as *sit* or *down*, reward him with a new, interesting toy.

Consult your veterinarian.

The truth is, your Sheltie will be a senior for at least half of his life, so obviously special senior care is important! Every senior Sheltie should have a health checkup every six months and be treated, fed, housed, and exercised according to *his* unique, specific needs.

Dogs have benefited greatly from medical and veterinary research and recent advances in health care. Dogs live longer today because they have access to better nutrition, veterinary care, immunizations, parasite control, and medications than what was available to them years ago. Dog owners are more informed about their pets today as well, more vigilant about their care, and more sensitive to their needs. All this leads to longer, happier, healthier lives for our canine companions.

Helpful Hints

Aging Eyes

Eye problems must be diagnosed by a veterinarian to determine the extent of visual impairment and whether the problems are age related.

- Lenticular sclerosis (also called nuclear sclerosis): transparent, grayish-blue haze that is a hardening of the lens within the eye. It is a normal sign of aging and usually starts to develop around six years of age. It does not disrupt vision.

- Cataracts: opaque, white area within the lens of the eye. Vision may be mildly or seriously impaired. Different types of cataracts can occur at different life stages. Some cataracts are inherited, and some may be seen with certain health problems, such as diabetes. Some cataracts can be removed, depending on the type.

Neither you, nor your veterinarian, can *prevent* the normal aging process, but there are things you both can do to *slow* the progression of health problems in your Sheltie caused by aging. You can do a lot to enrich your Sheltie's quality of life, too, so that he ages gracefully and comfortably in his golden years.

Surely the best and kindest thing you can do for your senior Sheltie is to continue to give him as much time, attention, and love throughout his life as you did when he was a puppy. Senior Shelties are polite and patient. They are not busy underfoot or demanding lots of attention and play activities in the same way puppies do. As a result of their quiet, good manners, old dogs are often taken for granted and do not receive the attention and care they *deserve.* Your senior Sheltie has been a loyal and devoted friend for years. He needs your love and care now just as much as he did when you first brought him home. Spend as much time as you can with him, and make sure he knows how special he is to you every day.

Sheltie are puppies at heart, no matter how old they are. As your Sheltie ages, he may initially be unaware of the gradual restrictions and limitations of an aging body. Although he can no longer run and play as hard as he did when he was young, he may still try, and when he does, injury can result. This is because aging gradually causes some degree of arthritis (painful joints), muscle weakness, and atrophy, leading to limited

movement and imbalance. As a result, things that were once easy to do may now be dangerous, such as running, jumping, or going up and down stairs. If your Sheltie has painful, limited, stiff movement in one or more joints, consult your veterinarian. Arthritis doesn't necessarily mean your pet can no longer enjoy going on walks with you, but it might be time to reduce the distance and pace and take more rest breaks along the way. Two or three short walks a day is better than one long, fast-paced, strenuous walk.

As your pet ages, his body's metabolic rate slows. This can lead to weight gain, an increased workload on the heart, a weaker heart, a reduction in organ function (especially liver and kidneys), muscle weakening and shrinkage, and a gradual overall deterioration in his health and condition. This decline in health is often accompanied by a decreased resistance to diseases, or immune suppression, and can be caused or worsened by stress.

Shelties are naturally gentle, good-natured dogs that adore their people. If

Breed Truths

Shelties have long life spans and can live well into their teens. Senior Shelties should have a health checkup every six months.

CAUTION

Contact your veterinarian immediately if your Sheltie shows any signs of behavioral change, or if he refuses to eat or drink, or if he appears to be in pain or discomfort.

your Sheltie is suddenly irritable with you or other members of your family, or seeks isolation, or seems disoriented, these are signs of a serious problem. Your Sheltie may be very sick or in pain. Strange behavioral changes can also indicate senility or cognitive dysfunction.

Aging is influenced by many factors, including health, genetics, nutrition, environment, hormones, and the type of care received throughout life. You may not have control over all of these factors, but there are two important things you can do to detect your Sheltie's problem and help slow its progression:

1. Take your Sheltie for a veterinary examination every six months.
2. As soon as you notice that your Sheltie has a problem or is not behaving normally, do not wait. Take him to a veterinarian right away.

Is Your Sheltie Confused?

No matter how old your Sheltie is, he will always want to please you. So, if he doesn't respond to a command, it may because he didn't hear you well, or perhaps didn't hear you at all. Maybe his eyesight is poor and he didn't see you. It is also possible that his memory is not as sharp as it used to be and he doesn't quite remember what he is expected to do, or he is confused. Many kinds of illness can cause mental confusion (hypothyroidism, diabetes, brain tumor). If your Sheltie is not responding to you as he normally does, it is likely a sign that something is wrong and that he needs to see a veterinarian to identify the problem.

Breed Truths

Changes in your aging Sheltie's lifestyle can be very stressful for him, especially if he is losing his hearing or sight. Try not to change his daily routine, food, exercise schedule, or environment. If you leave on vacation, ask a family member or friend to care for your Sheltie at your home so he can stay where he feels comfortable and secure and doesn't have to go to a boarding kennel.

Studies show that approximately one-third of dogs over the age of 11 develop some symptoms of canine cognitive dysfunction. This is considered the canine equivalent of senior dementia and is similar in some respects to Alzheimer's Disease in humans in the manner in which the brain cells are destroyed.

Canine cognitive dysfunction is characterized by confusion and disorientation. Other behavioral changes include decreased awareness, aimless wandering, barking and whining for no reason, panting, restlessness, getting "lost" behind doors and furniture, having elimination "accidents" in the house, changes in sleep patterns, aggression, depression, not recognizing family members and friends, and decreased responsiveness. At this time there is no specific test for canine cognitive dysfunction, nor is there a cure. Prescription medication is available for dogs to help slow the disease, lessen symptoms, and improve quality of life.

Stress Reduction

CAUTION

Older dogs take longer to recover from injury or illness than younger dogs.

One of the best things you can do for your Sheltie is reduce or prevent stress. As your Sheltie ages, he will become more sensitive to stress. Stress can make him more prone to illness, especially if he has a suppressed immune system, as many geriatric dogs do.

Shelties are stoic dogs and hide pain and illness very well. If your Sheltie has arthritis or some other painful condition, it is important to relieve his discomfort. Pain can stress your Sheltie to the point that he may be irritable, unable to sleep, unable to move normally, lose interest in food, and lose weight.

CHECKLIST

Keeping Your Senior Sheltie Comfortable

✔ Senior Shelties are more sensitive to abrupt changes in temperature and temperature extremes. Keep your pet at a comfortable temperature. Don't let him become overheated or chilled. Some senior Shelties may have thinner coats or hair loss. Make sure your Sheltie has a comfortable, warm bed in a draft-free area in which to sleep. Arthritis is more painful in cold weather.

✔ Give your Sheltie a soft bed made of natural products (cotton, wool). A foam cushion underneath the bed makes it more comfortable and helps retain warmth.

✔ Make sure your Sheltie has a non-slip, soft surface on which to rise, stand, and walk. Hard surfaces hurt old joints.

✔ Weigh your Sheltie once every month to be sure he is at a correct weight and not gaining or losing weight. Overweight dogs have more health problems.

✔ When you take your Sheltie for walks, let *him* set the pace. Leisurely, short walks are better for senior dogs than strenuous, extended walks. Walk your Sheltie on level, soft, nonslippery surfaces, such as grass or sand, when possible. Avoid hills, steep slopes, and stairs. Provide a ramp for your Sheltie to replace short flights of stairs. Keep his toenails trimmed.

✔ Feed a diet appropriate for your Sheltie's age and health condition. Feed small, frequent, nutritious meals, according to his activity level and needs. Senior Shelties can benefit from a high-protein diet. Consult your veterinarian about the best diet for your Sheltie.

✔ Feed your senior Sheltie two or three times a day. This helps your pet digest his food more easily. If he has gastrointestinal problems, feed him a bland diet.

✔ If your Sheltie has dental problems, make sure the food particles are small enough and soft enough to eat.

✔ Feed your Sheltie a high-quality diet appropriate for his age, health condition, teeth, and activity level. Ask your veterinarian about prescription diets available to treat, improve, or help prevent specific medical conditions.

✔ Make sure plenty of fresh water is available for your Sheltie at all times. If your Sheltie doesn't drink enough, he will be more prone to dehydration, electrolyte imbalance, bladder infections, kidney stones, and many other health problems.

✔ Take your Sheltie to your veterinarian at least once every six months for a complete physical examination to detect health problems early. Laboratory tests are necessary to monitor certain health conditions, such as diabetes, hypothyroidism, and anemia.

✔ Take your Sheltie out often to urinate and defecate. Senior Shelties cannot control their bladder and bowels as well as young dogs.

Your Sheltie may also be challenged by failing eyesight, poor hearing, or both. He may have difficulty distinguishing sounds, or where they originate. Because of these sensory losses, he may be easily startled, and that is very stressful, too.

Do not be surprised if your Sheltie no longer shares your enthusiasm for travel. As dogs age, they often tend to prefer to stay at home and rest where they feel safe. Travel can be very stressful for older dogs, especially if they are disoriented and cannot see and hear well.

A highly stressful situation for most dogs, senior or not, is being housed in a boarding kennel. Whether the boarding is at a commercial kennel facility or a veterinary hospital, these environments are not a "home away from home." They are often noisy and a likely place to contract contagious diseases, especially respiratory and intestinal diseases. When you must go away, let your Sheltie stay at home where he feels comfortable and secure. Ask a fam-

Helpful Hints

Ramps

As your Sheltie ages, it will be more difficult for him to climb stairs, get in and out of the car, or be on the sofa (if that is permitted!). A safe, nonslip ramp (available from pet stores) can help your Sheltie safely access these areas. Using a ramp will help prevent him from putting excess stress on his joints and straining his muscles. It will also help reduce the risk of injury caused by jumping or falling.

159

ily member or friend to pet-sit or come to your home at least three times daily to care for your Sheltie. Ideally, the person who takes care of him should be someone whom he knows and who is willing to spend time to visit with him. If you are going to be away for a long time, ask someone to live at your house with your Sheltie during your absence so he will not be too lonely or bored. It is better and safer for your Sheltie, too, because if he happens to fall ill while you are gone, there will be someone with him who can contact you and your veterinarian and take care of him immediately.

Helpful Hints

Senior Shelties have a high dietary protein requirement. Studies have shown that an increase in protein quality and quantity can be very beneficial for some geriatric dogs and may have anti-cancer and anti-diabetes effects.

Information for the Dog Sitter

Be sure to leave the dog sitter the following information:

1. A phone number where you can be reached in case of questions or emergency
2. A detailed list of care and feeding instructions and any special concerns
3. A list of any medications to give, the amount, and the times to give them
4. Your veterinarian's name, address, and phone number
5. The name, address, and phone number of the nearest veterinary emergency hospital
6. A signed document saying that the dog sitter has your permission to act as your agent/representative to take your Sheltie to the veterinary hospital for care
7. The name and number of an alternate contact in case of emergency, if you cannot return home as scheduled, or if the dog sitter cannot take care of your Sheltie the entire time you are absent
8. The location of the first aid kit

What About a Friend?

You may think adding a new puppy or dog to the family will revitalize your senior Sheltie, keep him company, entertain him, prevent boredom, and encourage him to exercise and play. It's possible, but it depends on many things, including your relationship with your Sheltie, his acceptance of other dogs, his age, health, and personality, and the family environment. Adding a new puppy is a decision that must be made very carefully.

It is possible that a new puppy might be good for you, too. If you are unable to imagine living in a house without a dog in it, the newcomer will help lessen your grief when the sad, but inevitable, time comes when you must say farewell to your precious senior companion.

If your Sheltie is not extremely old, or sick, he may welcome the friendship and activities of a new puppy—as long as the puppy doesn't get all the attention from you! If you add a new puppy to your home, it is very important that your Sheltie know he is still the top dog and has not lost his place in your heart. Always give him *lots* of attention and affection first, *before* the puppy. This assures your Sheltie that he is still loved and important, so he won't be jealous of the new arrival.

Supervise the interactions between your dogs to be sure they are compatible, but do not force your Sheltie to interact with the puppy. He will make friends in his own time and on his own terms. In addition, make sure that the energetic new puppy doesn't torment your Sheltie, steal his toys, take over his bed, or eat his food. Your Sheltie should always have a quiet place to retreat to where he can get away when he is tired of the puppy's activities. Make sure that the puppy's shenanigans do not irritate your sage senior!

Chapter Ten

Special Considerations

Should Your Sheltie Be Neutered?

One of the most important health decisions you will make for your Sheltie is whether to have him neutered. Neutering, more scientifically referred to as gonadectomy, is the removal of the gonads, the tissues in the body associated with reproduction: testicles in the male, ovaries and uterus in the female.

Female Shetland Sheepdogs usually come into estrus ("in heat" or "in season") around the age of 6 to 10 months and may cycle every 6 to 10 months throughout life. Estrous cycles vary according to family genetics. Male Shetland Sheepdogs may be sexually mature and able to reproduce by 10 months of age.

Historically, and until recently, dog owners (of all breeds and mixed breeds) were routinely advised to have their dogs neutered early in life. One of the main reasons for this recommendation was to reduce the number of accidental matings and unwanted pets in animal shelters. In addition, research has shown that neutering dogs can offer several medical benefits. For example, females spayed before their first estrous cycle have a significantly reduced chance of developing mammary (breast) cancer later in life. Mammary cancer is not unusual in older dogs and can be life-threatening. An ovariohysterectomy also eliminates the chances of having cancer, inflammation, infections, or other diseases of the uterus or ovaries. In males, neutering (castration) eliminates the risk of testicular and epididymal cancer and helps relieve or prevent some prostatic problems. Neutering has also been credited with reducing aggression and some behavioral problems in males.

Very early neutering of puppies was formally approved by the American Veterinary Medical Association (AVMA) in 1993. Studies showed that pre-pubertal gonadectomy on pups under 16 weeks of age did not affect growth rate, food intake, or weight gain of growing dogs, although some delay in epiphyseal closure of the long bones was documented.

FYI: Terminology

Gonadectomy: the removal of some, or all, of the tissues in the body associated with reproduction (castration or ovariohysterectomy)

Castration: removal of testicles, commonly called "neuter"

Ovariohysterectomy: removal of ovaries and uterus, commonly called "spay"

In the 20 years after the AVMA's approval of early neutering, additional studies indicate that although there are benefits of neutering, there are also long-term disadvantages that must now be taken into consideration, and that neutering may cause problems later in a dog's life. For example, it has long been known that females that have been spayed can develop some degree of urinary incontinence in their senior years (this problem can be treated with medication). There is now medical evidence that females that keep their ovaries live longer than those that have their ovaries removed, and that animals that have been neutered may be more prone to some kinds of cancer. These cases indicate that neutering may not be the best choice for all animals.

The fact is, *no medical or surgical procedure is ever completely without risk, and every case is different.*

Clearly, whether or not to neuter your Sheltie is a very important health decision that must be made carefully. Current legislative efforts in some localities to make it a *requirement* for pet owners to spay or neuter their dogs (*mandatory* spay/neuter laws) would prevent you and your veterinarian from making this important health decision together.

Consult with your veterinarian about the benefits and risks of neutering your Sheltie, *based on his age, health, and individual case.*

FYI: Just in Case

If you want to have your male Sheltie neutered but think you may one day want a litter of puppies from him, you do have an option. You can have your male's semen collected, frozen, and stored by a canine sperm bank before your dog is castrated (see "Resources") and later use the semen for artificial insemination. This is what many dog breeders have been doing successfully for decades. When canine sperm is stored in liquid nitrogen, it keeps for decades, if not indefinitely.

Travel

Whether you are socializing your Sheltie, participating in canine activities, or going on a trip, there will surely be significant travel involved.

- Make sure your Sheltie is trained to a crate and feels comfortable and secure inside of it *before* you take your trip. Crate training begins early in life, by using the crate as a security den. When it comes time to take a trip, your Sheltie should already feel at home in his crate.
- Obtain a health certificate for travel. Make sure your pet is in excellent health and able to make the trip. Ask your veterinarian to do a physical examination, verify that all necessary vaccinations are up to date, and sign a health certificate for travel. Ask if any special medications for the trip are recommended (for example, medication for the prevention of heartworm, or medication for car sickness).
- Make reservations in advance.
- Check with hotels or campgrounds to be sure pets are permitted.
- Reserve space for your dog with the airlines if you are traveling by air.

Helpful Hints

Travel Tips

1. Train your Sheltie to a crate (travel kennel) early. Start when he is a puppy.
2. Make a few short practice trips, even if it's just driving around the block.
3. Obtain a health certificate for out-of-state travel.
4. Make reservations well in advance, and advise hotels and airlines you are traveling with a pet.
5. Allow your pet to have a drink of bottled water every few hours to prevent dehydration.
6. Make a list of everything you will need and pack well in advance.

Travel by Air

Only a limited number of animals may travel on a given flight, either in the cabin or in the cargo hold, so make your reservation as early as you can. The cargo hold is temperature controlled and pressurized just like the cabin in which you travel. With heightened airline security, it takes longer to check dogs in for flights, so arrive at the airport early. Ask the airline company what their specific requirements are so that you will have everything in order and be prepared *before* you arrive at the airport.

For your Sheltie's comfort, and your peace of mind, book direct flights when possible, and do not travel during extreme weather conditions or major holidays, when flights may be delayed or canceled. Put labels on the flight crate with your name and contact information at home and at the

CHECKLIST

Traveling Supplies

- ✔ Travel crate (airlines require plastic or aluminum crate: doors and screws must be metal)
- ✔ Leash
- ✔ Collar with identification tag
- ✔ Dishes, food, and bottled water
- ✔ Medications
- ✔ First aid kit

- ✔ Toys and bedding from home
- ✔ Grooming supplies
- ✔ Cleanup equipment: pooper scooper, plastic bags, paper towels, hand sanitizer, moistened disinfectant wipes
- ✔ Veterinary records, photo identification, microchip number, and contact phone numbers

point of destination, the flight number, and your Sheltie's name and breed. Place towels or blankets in the crate for bedding, and securely attach the food and water dishes. To minimize spills, you can freeze the water in your pet's dish. It is helpful to fasten a water bottle on the outside of the crate door with the sipper tube directly over the water dish so your Sheltie has plenty to drink during the trip. Secure the top and bottom of the crate, and the door, with zip ties.

Note: Tranquilizers are not recommended for air travel. They can cause death at high altitudes and may inhibit proper body temperature regulation.

CAUTION

Never leave your Sheltie in a parked car on a hot day, even for a few minutes. The temperature inside a car, even with the windows cracked open and parked in the shade, can quickly soar past 120°F (49°C) within a few short minutes, and your pet can rapidly die of heatstroke.

Airlines will not accept sedated animals. In addition, some common tranquilizers may be toxic for Shelties if they carry the MDR1 gene (see the section on the MDR1 gene later in the chapter).

Travel by Car

Some dogs are prone to car sickness, especially when they are young. To reduce the likelihood that your Sheltie will be carsick, limit his food three hours before travel. If possible, place his crate where he can see outside of the car. Although some dogs become carsick from anxiety about travel, tranquilizers are not always effective in preventing car sickness, nor are they always recommended. Ask your veterinarian about prescribing a safe anti-nausea medication for your Sheltie. Always check first with your veterinarian before giving your pet any medications.

Shetland Sheepdog Health Problems

The Shetland Sheepdog is a strong, robust, long-lived breed with few medical problems. However, all dog breeds have certain medical conditions to which they are more predisposed than others. Responsible Sheltie breeders go to great lengths to test their dogs for possible genetic problems (when tests are available), and the Shetland Sheepdog national, state, and local clubs continually have ongoing research projects to identify, test for, and ultimately eliminate diseases that may be inherited in Shelties.

The Canine Health Information Center (CHIC) (*www.caninehealthinfo.org*) is a centralized canine health data base jointly sponsored by the American Kennel Club Canine Health Foundation (AKC/CHF) and the Orthopedic Foundation for Animals (OFA). Its mission statement is "To provide a source of health information for owners, breeders, and scientists, that will assist in breeding healthy dogs."

Among the many CHIC objectives are to work with breed clubs to identify health issues, to maintain a central information system to support research into canine disease, and to provide information to owners and breeders. Information on individually identified dogs is available at the consent of the owner.

For each breed, specific tests are required. Dogs of each breed that have been tested receive a CHIC number. For dog buyers, the CHIC program provides accurate information about the breeder's health tests on individual dogs. For a Shetland Sheepdog to receive a CHIC number, it must have had the following tests:

Required:

1. Hip dysplasia: OFA evaluation or PennHIP evaluation
2. Eye clearance: CERF evaluation. Evaluation recommended every year until five years of age, then every two years thereafter until nine years of age.

Two electives from the following:

1. vWD (von Willebrand's Disease test) with results registered with the OFA.
2. MDR1 test at Washington State University Clinical Pharmacology Laboratory with results registered with the OFA.
3. OFA Thyroid evaluation from an approved laboratory. Recommend testing at two, four, and seven years of age.
4. Collie eye anomaly (CEA) test by Optigen with test results registered with the OFA.
5. OFA elbow dysplasia evaluation

Optional tests:

1. Congenital Cardiac Database: test recommended to be performed by a board certified cardiologist or board-certified specialist in internal medicine.

Sheltie breeders, clubs, and veterinary colleges and universities are continually investigating canine health problems. The following health problems are not limited to Shelties. These problems can affect other breeds, including mixed breeds, so the dedicated work of the Sheltie enthusiasts benefits many.

It is unlikely that your Sheltie has any of the conditions listed below, but if he does, this list will help you to recognize the problem, so you can seek veterinary help.

Eye Problems

The following are eye disorders proven or suspected to be hereditary in Shetland Sheepdogs, listed by the American College of Veterinary Ophthalmologists.

Choroidal Hypoplasia (CH), also commonly referred to as Sheltie Eye Syndrome (SES) or Collie Eye Anomaly (CEA)

Choroidal hypoplasia (CH) is an inherited autosomal recessive disorder, meaning both parents must be carriers of the gene to produce affected offspring. CH occurs in several herding breeds. It is an inadequate development of the choroid, present at birth. It does not progress in severity with age. It can vary from mild with little to no visual impairment, to severe with partial or total loss of vision. The degree of severity can vary in each eye.

Helpful Hints

A DNA test is available (see "Resources") to identify a normal-eyed dog (non-carrier of the CH gene); a dog that carries one gene for the condition (is heterozygous for CH); or a dog affected with the disorder (is homozygous and carries two genes for CH).

FYI: Eye Examination

The Canine Eye Registration Foundation (CERF) tracks eye diseases in dogs and registers dogs examined and certified by veterinary ophthalmologic specialists as being free of heritable eye diseases. The dog is examined by an ophthalmologist, who fills out a special form and gives a copy to the owner. The owner can send the copy to CERF with the registration fee to receive a CERF registration number. Registration is good for one year and must be renewed annually by examination, to maintain an up-to-date CERF number.

The ophthalmologic examination checks

- eyeball size, shape, anatomy, and color;
- eye movement;
- cornea, lens, iris, pupils;
- the interior and back of the eye ;
- intraocular pressure; and
- eyelids and lashes.

Conscientious Sheltie breeders have their puppies examined by a veterinary ophthalmologist *before* they place their puppies in homes.

The choroid is a layer of tissue underneath the retina. Dogs affected with CH have thin, underdeveloped choroids with reduced pigmentation. Blood vessels in the choroid are also reduced in number and may be abnormally shaped. In severe CH, there can be clefts, or "pits" in the choroid, leading to impaired vision in the affected eye.

An ophthalmologic examination is needed to diagnose CH and its severity. In merle Shelties, especially those with blue eyes or partially blue eyes, care must be taken to differentiate lack of pigmentation caused by CH from normal eyes with less pigmentation caused by the influence of the merle gene.

Progressive Retinal Atrophy There are different types of progressive retinal atrophy. Central progressive atrophy has been identified in Shelties. It is an autosomal recessive degenerative condition of the retinal visual cells that eventually progresses to

Breed Truths

According to the Canine Eye Registration Foundation's most recent report, the incidence of CH in Shelties presented for examination in the United States is relatively low at about .39 percent. This figure reflects only the animals that were examined. It is unknown what percentage of the Sheltie population has been examined and what the incidence may be among Shelties that were not examined.

blindness. At this time a DNA test for CPRA for Shelties is not yet available. Affected animals can be diagnosed by electroretinogram before symptoms develop. There is no cure.

Distichiasis Distichiasis is the abnormal location of eyelashes in the eyelid margin. Shelties with distichiasis usually have stiff hairs that require surgical removal so they do not irritate the surface of the eye. Distichiasis can occur any time during life.

Persistent Pupillary Membranes Persistent pupillary membranes (PPM) are remnants of blood vessels in the anterior chamber of the eye that failed to regress normally in the newborn. PPM may be of little to no medical significance, or they may cause visual impairment, depending on where the remnant strands are attached.

Corneal Dystrophy Corneal dystrophy is a noninflammatory opacity present in one or more layers of the cornea. It is usually inherited and usually present in both eyes. In some Shelties, corneal dystrophy may lead to an erosion of the cornea. Therapy (artificial tears and other treatments) is needed to keep the animal comfortable.

Cataract A cataract is a lens opacity that may affect one or both eyes and may cause partial or complete blindness. Depending on the type of cataract, it may be possible to surgically remove.

Hip Dysplasia

Hip dysplasia starts in immature dogs with an instability, or a loose fit, of the hip joint (where the head of the femur fits into the acetabulum of the pelvis). The joint laxity causes abnormal movement in the joint, and abnormal wear of joint cartilage, deforms the acetabulum, and results in pain and lameness. Over time, osteophytes (bone spurs) form, leading to osteoarthritis and degenerative joint disease. This damages the joint and results in pain and lameness. Symptoms can range from mild to severe, and diagnosis is made by clinical examination together with radiographs (X rays).

171

Causes of hip dysplasia are multiple and include genetic and environmental influences. Fortunately, hip dysplasia is not as common a problem in Shelties in the United States as it is in most other breeds. According to the Orthopedic Foundation for Animals statistics gathered from 1974 through 2010, of more than 18,000 Shelties examined, more than 25 percent of them had excellent hip ratings, and less than 5 percent were affected with hip dysplasia (*www.offa.org/stat_hip.html*). Sheltie breeders continue to screen for hip dysplasia in an effort to eliminate it completely from the breed.

Dental Abnormalities

1. "Lance" canine teeth: abnormal placement of the upper canine tooth. The tooth is displaced forward and comes in contact with the third upper incisor, rather than being placed behind the lower canine tooth as it should be.
2. Abnormal size, shape, or position of third upper incisor (one or both).

Fun Facts

Mitochondrial DNA research has shown that the MDR1 gene mutation occurred long ago, before contemporary breeds existed (before 1873) and as early as 40 to 120 generations before the development of contemporary breeds. DNA research also showed that all of the breeds that carry the MDR1 gene share a single common ancestor!

Dermatomyositis (DM)

DM is a genetic disease of skin and muscle that can cause skin lesions with or without hair loss, redness, scaling, and crusting. Lesions appear on one or more of the following: the face, ears, legs, feet, and tip of tail. Some animals may suffer from muscular weakness, although muscle involvement in Shelties is rare. The condition is believed to be of complex inheritance and triggered by various factors, including hormonal fluctuations and stress. Diagnosis is confirmed by biopsy. Medication is available for treatment. Studies are under way to determine the cause and inheritance of DM.

Multi-drug Resistance Gene (MDR1)

Some breeds, particularly among the herding breeds, are more sensitive to certain drugs than other breeds. This is caused by a mutation in a gene that encodes for a protein responsible for pumping drugs and toxins out of the brain. Dogs that have this mutant gene, called the multi-drug resistance gene (MDR1), are unable to pump some drugs out of the brain in the same way other dogs can. This results in illness and abnormal neurologic signs, and sometimes leads to death.

According to the Washington State University College of Veterinary Medicine, 15 percent of Shetland Sheepdogs carry the MDR1 gene. This is low compared with some herding breeds, such as the Sheltie's close relative the Collie, in which 70 percent of the population carries the gene.

FYI: Drug Interactions

Drugs that can cause problems in dogs that carry the MDR1 gene:

1. **Acepromazine:** tranquilizer and pre-anesthetic agent
2. **Butorphanol:** analgesic and pre-anesthetic agent
3. **Emodepside (Profender):** deworming drug
4. **Erythromycin:** antibiotic
5. **Ivermectin, selamectin, milbemycin, moxidectin :** anti-parasitic drugs, also used as heartworm preventive. These drugs must be used cautiously. Do not exceed the recommended dose!
6. **Loperamide (Imodium):** anti-diarrheal agent
7. **Vincristine, Vinblastine, Doxorubicin:** chemotherapy agents

As more research is conducted, it is likely that more drugs will be added to this list.

It is important to have your Sheltie tested to find out if he carries the MDR1 gene, so you can know if he might be sensitive to certain drugs. The DNA test can be done using either cells taken from the inside of the cheek or using a blood sample. You can order a test kit directly from Washington State Veterinary College at *www.vetmed.wsu.edu/depts-VCPL/test.aspx*.

von Willebrand Disease

von Willebrand disease (vWD) is a congenital, inherited bleeding disorder that affects more than 50 breeds of dogs. It is a disease of platelet dysfunction that leads to excessive bleeding after injury or trauma, bruising, and delayed blood clotting time. Shelties rank among the top seven breeds most commonly affected with vWD.

The disease is recessive, so both parents must carry the gene to produce affected offspring. Breeders check their Shelties to know if they are genetic carriers for vWD. Genetic carriers for vWD should not be bred.

A DNA test is available directly from VetGen and requires only a cheek-cell swab to be submitted (*www.vetgen.com/ordertests*).

The American Shetland Sheepdog Association continues research into other conditions that affect Shelties (and other breeds). For example, Shelties have a higher incidence of transitional cell carcinoma of the bladder than most other breeds. In addition, gall bladder mucocele (an abnormally distended gall bladder containing a buildup of mucus) is known to affect Shelties with a higher incidence than most other breeds. With the assistance of the American Shetland Sheepdog Association, researchers have identified a genetic mutation responsible for the problem. These research findings will benefit other dog breeds, as well as humans.

Deafness and Microphthalmia

Inherited deafness and microphthalmia (small or underdeveloped eyes) in Shelties can occur in animals that carry two merle genes (homozygous merles, also known as white-merles, or "double dilutes"). These dogs are easy to identify. Their heads and bodies are almost entirely white. They can be unilaterally or bilaterally deaf. In some cases they may also suffer from microphthalmia or anophthalmia (absence of eyes). Extensive research is under way to understand the complexities of how specific genes associated with coloration, especially the merle and piebald genes, can affect hearing.

Most Sheltie breeders do not breed merle Shelties together, nor do they place white-merle puppies in pet homes, so it is unlikely that you will encounter this problem.

Problem Barking

Problem barking is when your dog barks incessantly, or for no apparent reason, and the barking has reached a point that it annoys you and possibly your neighbors. Like most behavioral problems, prevention is easier than correction. If you discourage excessive barking when your Sheltie

BE PREPARED! Teaching Your Sheltie Quiet and Speak

1. When your Sheltie barks, get his attention by clapping or whistling or making a sound.
2. When he stops barking, say "*Quiet*" in a firm but upbeat tone while giving him a food reward.
3. Practice the *quiet* command often throughout the day, whenever your Sheltie barks.
4. Have a supply of treats readily available in your pocket throughout these training sessions.
5. Rewards must be given immediately for them to be effective.
6. Make sure your pet knows he is being rewarded for being quiet and not for barking!
7. You should keep the training session short, but you can repeat it several times throughout the day.

After your Sheltie has learned *quiet*, you can teach him the *bark* command.
1. Have someone knock on the door, ring a doorbell, or do something that would normally cause your dog to bark.
2. As soon as your Sheltie barks, say "*Bark*" in a happy voice and give him a food reward.
3. When your Sheltie has *learned the two commands separately and knows the difference*, ask him to bark, then tell him to be quiet and give him a reward *immediately*.

is a puppy, and reward him when he is quiet, he will learn early on that excessive barking is unacceptable. However, if you think his puppy barking is cute and let him bark as much as he wants, whenever he wants, he will keep that behavior into adulthood and be confused when you try to discipline him. Also, if you shout at him to be quiet when he is barking, he will interpret your shouts as giving him attention and your way of joining in on the noise making.

There are as many ways to deal with problem barking as there are barking dogs. If your Sheltie's barking has become a serious problem that you cannot manage, consult a veterinary behaviorist or a trainer for guidance in behavioral-modification techniques. (Behavior modification should be tried before bark collars. Also, bark collars often do not work.)

One method that has proved successful in some cases is to teach your pet two commands. One is to *bark* or *speak* on command and the other command is to *hush* or be *quiet*. The same word should be used each time. The *quiet* command is not easy to teach. It may take several weeks to learn and requires patience and perseverance. *A key component to successful training is to reward your pet immediately when he does the right thing*!

10 **Questions** About Sheltie Health and Behavior ▬▬▬

1 **My Sheltie barks a lot. What can I do?** Shelties can be enthusiastic barkers, as are many herding dogs. However, if your Sheltie barks excessively, or for no apparent reason, then he needs to learn that this behavior is unacceptable. He also needs to learn to stop barking when you tell him to stop, and this requires focused training. If excessive barking has become a problem you cannot manage, you can consult a veterinary behaviorist (visit *www.dacvb.org*) or a skilled trainer.

2 **How can my Sheltie stay cool on hot days?** If the outdoor temperature is too warm and uncomfortable for you, then it's too warm for your Sheltie, too. Keep him indoors where it is cooler on warm days. Your Sheltie should always have plenty of water and shade available at all times. Shelties cool down by panting. They also sweat through their footpads. Keep in mind that on a hot day, sidewalks, asphalt, and dirt paths can reach such high temperatures that they are too hot to touch. Your Sheltie can burn and injure his feet if he is forced to walk on these hot surfaces.

3 **Does my Sheltie really need medication to prevent heartworm disease?** If you are living in, or traveling to, a state where heartworm exists, your Sheltie definitely needs protection! Prevention is much easier, safer, and more successful than treatment for heartworm disease. First, your veterinarian will do a heartworm test to be sure your pet is free of the disease. Then a once-a-month medication can be prescribed to keep him safe. There are several products available for heartworm prevention that are safe for Shelties. Consult your veterinarian.

4 **What is temperament testing?** Temperament tests assess a dog's mental stability in a variety of situations. Different tests are used and measured according to a breed's inherent tendencies. The tests evaluate aspects such as friendliness, shyness, protectiveness, fear, and aggression in everyday-life situations. Tests can include walking in a park, going through a crowd, meeting other animals, and encountering strangers and children. Temperament testing appraises a dog's ability to recognize nonthreatening and threatening situations and how a dog responds to them. (For more information, visit *www.atts.org*.)

5 **Should I microchip my Sheltie?** Yes! Your Sheltie should definitely be microchipped! A microchip is a permanent and effective form of identification. It is a transponder about the size of a grain of rice implanted under the skin quickly and easily by injection. Each microchip has a unique series of numbers. A handheld scanner (reader, decoder) is used to read the identification numbers. If your Sheltie is ever lost or stolen, his microchip will be his ticket to reuniting with you, and it will be your proof that he truly belongs to you.

6 **Does my Sheltie really need to be vaccinated?** Yes, your Sheltie should be vaccinated! Every time your Sheltie encounters other dogs, or environments where other dogs have been—on a walk, at the park, in a boarding kennel, or at your veterinarian's—he is at risk for contracting deadly diseases. He will not be protected against these diseases unless he is vaccinated. Consult your veterinarian for a vaccine program designed specifically for your Sheltie's health, age, and risk of exposure.

7 **Should I neuter my Sheltie?** Whether to neuter or spay your Sheltie is one of the most important health decisions you will make for your pet. There are medical benefits, as well as some risks and disadvantages, associated with these procedures. Every animal is different. Your veterinarian can provide you with detailed information about the benefits and risks of neutering so that you can make the best health decision for your Sheltie, based on his age, health, and individual case.

8 **Can my Sheltie get sunburned?** Ultraviolet rays from the sun can cause painful sunburn, blistering, and crusting. It can also cause skin cancers in dogs, just as it does in humans. Shelties have a lot of hair, so your pet's body has more protection where the coat is thick. However, the top of the muzzle does not have much hair on it and is continually exposed, so it can sunburn, even on overcast days, especially in areas where the skin is not pigmented and the hair is white. The top of your pet's ears may also burn. You can protect your Sheltie from sunburn by using sunscreen approved specifically for pet use.

9 **My Sheltie has bad breath and plaque buildup on her teeth. What can I do?** Bacteria, plaque, and tartar buildup cause bad breath and lead to periodontal disease. If left untreated, bacteria can enter the bloodstream and cause illness, such as abscess formation in body organs or damage to heart valves. Ask your veterinarian to examine, clean, and polish your Sheltie's teeth. After your Sheltie's teeth are clean, continue brushing them at least once a week using a dentifrice developed for dogs.

10 **I keep my Sheltie groomed and clean, but sometimes I notice a foul odor under his tail. What is that, and what can I do about it?** All dogs have a pair of anal sacs on each side of the inside of the rectum. The sacs contain a bad-smelling brown liquid that is usually emptied during defecation. Sometimes the sacs become impacted and need to be manually expressed (emptied) by a veterinarian or groomer. Consult your veterinarian to make sure your Sheltie's anal sacs are not impacted, infected, abscessed, or ruptured.

Resources

Books

The Complete Dog Book: Official Publication of the American Kennel Club. New York: Howell Book House, 1992.

Carriera, Joanne. *Shetland Sheepdogs at Work*. Loveland, CO: Best Friends, 1999.

Clark, L. A., Wahl, J. M., Rees, C. A., Strain, G. M., Cargill, E. J., Vanderlip, S. L., Murphy, K. E. "Canine SINEs and Their Effects on Phenotypes of the Domestic Dog." *Genomics of Disease*. New York: Springer Science, 2008.

Coleman, Catherine E. *The Shetland Sheepdog*. New York: Mail and Express, 1943.

Combe, Iris. *Herding Dogs, Their Origins and Development in Britain*. London: Faber and Faber, 1987.

Coren, Stanley. *The Intelligence of Dogs. A Guide to the Thoughts, Emotions, and Inner Lives of Our Canine Companions*. New York: Free Press, 2006.

Hart, Malcolm. *Shetland Sheepdogs: An Owner's Companion*. Wiltshire, UK: The Crowood Press, 1999.

McKinney, Betty Jo and Rieseberg, Barbara. *Sheltie Talk*. Loveland, CO: Alpine Publications, 1985.

Norman, Margaret. *The Complete Shetland Sheepdog*. Gloucestershire, UK: Ringpress Books, 1998.

Vanderlip, Sharon, and Ludwig, Gert. *1000 Dog Names from A to Z*. Hauppauge, NY: Barron's Educational Series, 2005.

Vanderlip, Sharon. *The Collie— A Veterinary Reference for the Professional Breeder*. Cardiff by the Sea, CA: Biotechnical Veterinary Consultants, 1984.

Periodicals

AKC Gazette
(800) 533-7323
www.akc.org/pubs

AKC Family Dog
(800) 533-7323
www.akc.org/pubs

Dog Fancy
www.dogchannel.com/dog-magazines

Dog World
www.dogchannel.com/dog-magazines

Dogs USA Annual
www.dogchannel.com/dog-magazines

Sheltie International
P.O. Box 6369
Los Osos, CA 93412
(805) 528-2007
www.sheltieinternational.com

Sheltie Pacesetter
9428 Blue Mound Drive
Fort Wayne, IN 46804
(260) 434-1566
S.Pacesetter@sheltie.com
www.sheltie.com

Shetland Sheepdog–Related Organizations

American Kennel Club (AKC)
8051 Arco Corporate Drive, Suite 100
Raleigh, NC 27617-3390
(919) 233-9767
www.akc.org

American Shetland Sheepdog
  Association
www.assa.org

Canadian Kennel Club
89 Skyway Avenue, Suite 100
Etibicoke
Ontario, Canada M9W6R4
(416) 675-5511
www.ckc.ca

United Kennel Club
100 East Kilgore Road
Kalamazoo, MI 49001
(616) 343-9020
www.ukcdogs.com

Shetland Sheepdog Activities

Flyball
www.flyball.com

AKC
Good Citizen Program
www.akc.org/events/cgc/index.cfm

AKC Rally
www.akc.org/events/rally

AKC Agility
www.akc.org/events/agility

North American Dog Agility
  Council
11522 S. Highway 3
Cataldo, ID 83810
www.nadac.com

United States Dog Agility
  Association
P.O. Box 850955
Richardson, TX 75085
(972) 487-2200
www.usdaa.com

Therapy and Service

American Temperament Test
  Society, Inc.
P.O. Box 800130
Balch Springs, TX 75180
(972) 557-2887
info@atts.org
www.atts.org

Delta Society Pet Partners Program
(425) 226-7357
info@deltasociety.org
www.deltasociety.org

The Bright and Beautiful Therapy
  Dogs, Inc.
(888) PET-5770
info@golden-dogs.org
www.golden-dogs.org

Therapy Dogs International
(973) 252-9800
tdi@gti.net
www.tdi-dog.org

Therapy Dogs Incorporated
(877) 843-7364
therapydogs@sisna.com
www.therapydogs.com

National Association for Search
  and Rescue
4500 Southgate Place, Suite 100
Chantilly, VA 20157
(703) 222-6277
www.nasar.org

Shetland Sheepdog Rescue Information

www.akc.org/breeds/rescue
www.assa.org/rescue.html

Travel Information

United States Department of
    Agriculture
www.aphis.usda.gov/animal_welfare/
    pet_travel/pet_travel.shtml

American Kennel Club
www.akc.org/public_education/
    travel_tips.cfm

American Dog Owners Association
www.adoa.org

United States Department of
    Transportation
www.airconsumer.dot.gov/publications/
    animals.htm

Health-Related Associations and Foundations

AKC Canine Health Foundation
P.O. Box 900061
Raleigh, NC 27675-9061
(888) 682-9696
www.akcchf.org

American Veterinary Medical
    Association
930 North Meacham Road
Schaumberg, IL 60173
www.avma.org

Association of Pet Dog Trainers
150 Executive Center Drive, Box 35
Greenville, SC 29615
(800) PET-DOGS
information@apdt.com
www.apdt.com

Canine Eye Registration Foundation
www.vmdb.org/cerf.html

Orthopedic Foundation for Animals
www.offa.org

Canine Health Information Center
www.caninehealthinfo.org

International Canine Semen Bank
Main Office, Oregon
www.ik9sb.com

Information on Household Poisons

www.epa.gov
www.cdc.gov

Training and Behavior Websites

American College of Veterinary
    Behaviorists
www.veterinarybehaviorists.org

Animal Behavior Society
www.animalbehaviorsociety.org

Lost-Pet Registries

AKC Companion Recovery
5580 Centerview Drive, Suite 250
Raleigh, NC 27606-3394
(800) 252-7894
found@akc.org
www.akccar.org

Avid Identification Systems, Inc.
3185 Hamner Avenue
Norco, CA 92860
(800) 336-2843
www.avidid.com

Home Again Microchip Service
(888) HOME AGAIN
public.homeagain.com

Index

THE TEAM BEHIND THE *TRAIN YOUR DOG* DVD

Host **Nicole Wilde** is a certified Pet Dog Trainer and internationally recognized author and lecturer. Her books include *So You Want to Be a Dog Trainer* and *Help for Your Fearful Dog* (Phantom Publishing). In addition to working with dogs, Nicole has been working with wolves and wolf hybrids for over fifteen years and is considered an expert in the field.

Host **Laura Bourhenne** is a Professional Member of the Association of Pet Dog Trainers, and holds a degree in Exotic Animal Training. She has trained many species of animals including several species of primates, birds of prey, and many more. Laura is striving to enrich the lives of pets by training and educating the people they live with.

Director **Leo Zahn** is an award winning director/cinematographer/editor of television commercials, movies, and documentaries. He has directed and edited more than a dozen instructional DVDs through the Picture Company, a subsidiary of Picture Palace, Inc., based in Los Angeles.

The enclosed training DVD is provided as bonus material for the consumer. It is published independently, and therefore does not necessarily reflect the opinions, views, or practices of the author and/or Barron's Educational Series, Inc. Neither the author nor Barron's shall be held responsible for any injury, loss, expense, or damage suffered or incurred by any person or animal who participates in the training exercises demonstrated in the enclosed video presentation.